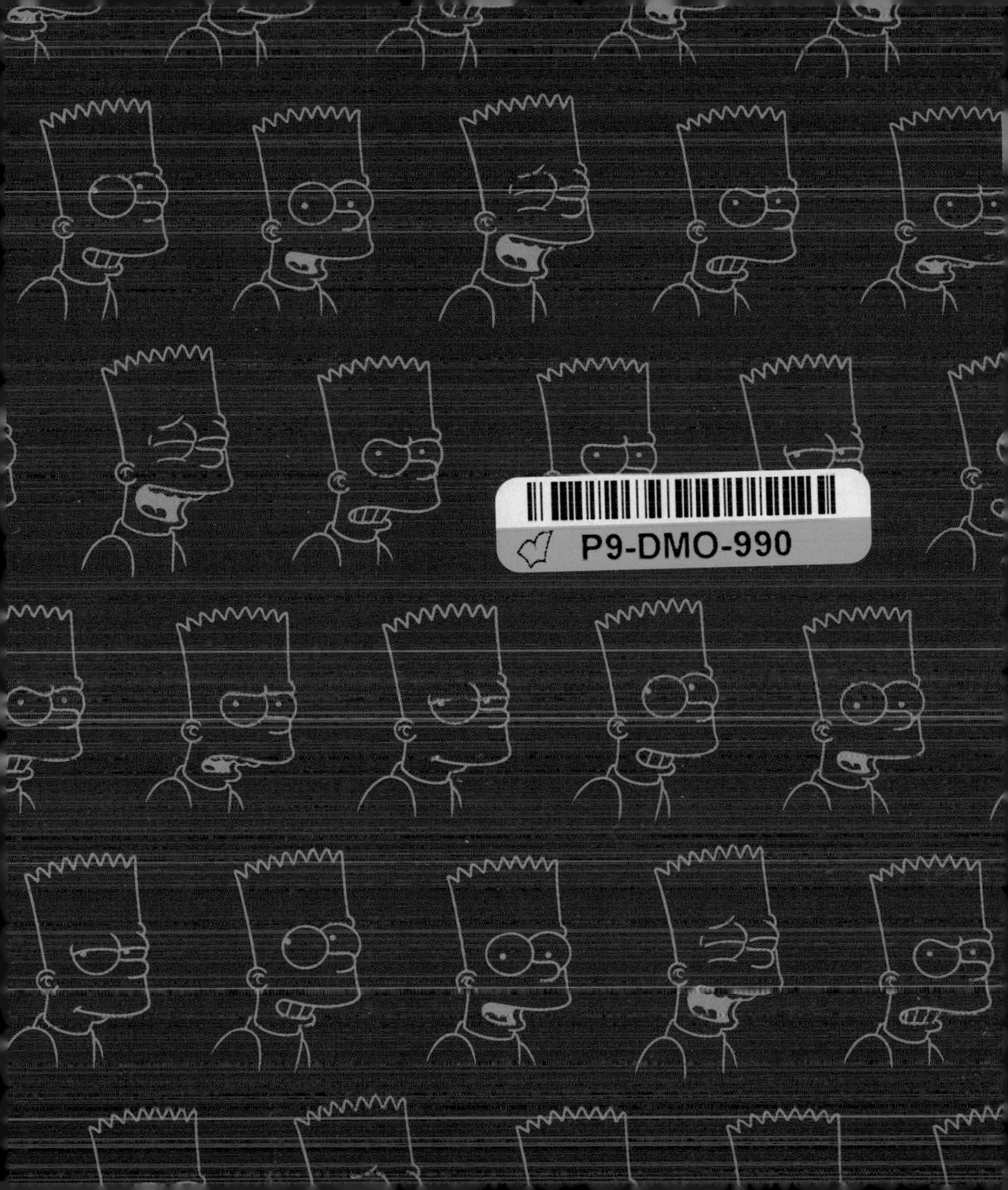

THE SIMPSONS™ LIBRARY OF WISDOM
THE BART BOOK

Copyright © 2004 by
Bongo Entertainment, Inc. and Matt Groening Productions, Inc. All rights reserved.

Printed in the United States of America.
No part of this book may be used or reproduced in any manner whatsoever without written permission
except in the case of brief quotations embodied in critical articles and reviews. For information address
HarperCollins Publishers Inc.,
10 East 53rd Street, New York, NY 10022.

HarperCollins books may be purchased for educational, business, or sales
promotional use. For information please write:
Special Markets Department,
HarperCollins Publishers Inc.,
10 East 53rd Street, New York, NY 10022.

FIRST EDITION

ISBN 0-06-073885-5

04 05 06 07 08 09 RRD 10 9 8 7 6 5 4 3 2 1

Publisher: Matt Groening
Creative Director: Bill Morrison
Managing Editor: Terry Delegeane
Director of Operations: Robert Zaugh
Art Director: Nathan Kane
Special Projects Art Director: Serban Cristescu
Production Manager: Christopher Ungar
Production/Design: Karen Bates, Art Villanueva
Staff Artists: Chia-Hsien Jason Ho, Mike Rote
Production Assistant: Nathan Hamill
Administration: Sherri Smith
Legal Guardian: Susan A. Grode

THE SIMPSONS™ LIBRARY OF WISDOM

Conceived and Edited by Bill Morrison
Book Design and Production by Serban Cristescu
Contributing Editor: Terry Delegeane
Research and Production Assistance: Nathan Hamill

Contributing Artists:
John Costanza, Serban Cristescu, Mike DeCarlo, John Delaney, Luis Escobar, Chia-Hsien Jason Ho,
William Mahaney, Bill Morrison, Kevin M. Newman, Mike Rote, Kevin Segna, Chris Ungar

Contributing Writers:
Jamie Angell, Scott M. Gimple, Nathan Hamill, Jesse L. McCann, Bill Morrison, Eric Rogers

HarperCollins Editors: Susan Weinberg, Kate Travers

Special Thanks to:
Pete Benson, N. Vyolet Diaz, Deanna MacLellan, Helio Salvatierra,
Mili Smythe, and Ursula Wendel

THE BART BOOK

Perennial
Currents
An Imprint of HarperCollins *Publishers*

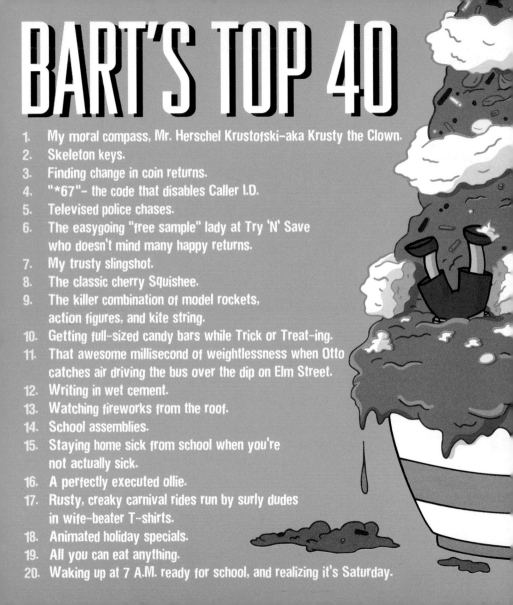

BART'S TOP 40

1. My moral compass, Mr. Herschel Krustofski–aka Krusty the Clown.
2. Skeleton keys.
3. Finding change in coin returns.
4. "*67"– the code that disables Caller I.D.
5. Televised police chases.
6. The easygoing "free sample" lady at Try 'N' Save who doesn't mind many happy returns.
7. My trusty slingshot.
8. The classic cherry Squishee.
9. The killer combination of model rockets, action figures, and kite string.
10. Getting full-sized candy bars while Trick or Treat-ing.
11. That awesome millisecond of weightlessness when Otto catches air driving the bus over the dip on Elm Street.
12. Writing in wet cement.
13. Watching fireworks from the roof.
14. School assemblies.
15. Staying home sick from school when you're not actually sick.
16. A perfectly executed ollie.
17. Rusty, creaky carnival rides run by surly dudes in wife-beater T-shirts.
18. Animated holiday specials.
19. All you can eat anything.
20. Waking up at 7 A.M. ready for school, and realizing it's Saturday.

21. Comic book conventions.
22. Radioactive Man #628: The ish where Radioactive Man uses the sun as a weapon against the Cosmic Commander, shouting, "Have a ball--of incomprehensibly hot nuclear energy!" (Genius! You can't make that stuff up!)
23. Ice cream on a hot summer day.
24. Ice cream on a freezing day.
25. Ice cream on a room-temperature day.
26. The flying monkeys in "Wizard of Oz" (Actually, pretty much monkeys in general).
27. Phlegm (also on my Bottom 40).
28. Clueless substitute teachers.
29. Seeing people mistake wasabi for guacamole.
30. The "Krusty's Kut-Out Klassics" DVD clip where a hot studio light falls on Sideshow Bob's head, causing his hair to burst into flames.
31. The beloved cartoon violence of "Itchy & Scratchy."
32. Making Milhouse laugh hard enough to make milk shoot out of his nose.
33. Snow forts.
34. Watching televised surgery during suppertime.
35. The triple deck, fat-fried, Jumbo Joke Funny Meal with medium seltzer at Krustyburger.
36. When Mom burns the salmon croquettes and we get to eat #35.
37. Truckasaurus.
38. The annual field trip to the "Ah, Fudge!" factory.
39. Getting Skinner's goat.
40. Playing catch in the yard with Homer. (Don't tell him!)

BART FROM THE START

AGE: MINUS 3 MONTHS
Still in womb, medical experts are surprised by Bart's apparent self-awareness. Many ultrasound moonings follow.

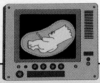

AGE: DAY ONE
After 53 hours of labor, baby Bart decides to come out. Mother Marge is exhausted; baby is alert and starting fires.

AGE: 6 MONTHS
Cast in commercials as "Baby Stinkbreath," Bart's early showbiz success /peak /decline further motivates him to seek negative attention. Nude clothesline swingings / keys, wallet, false teeth flushings follow.

AGE: 1 YEAR, 4 MONTHS
Bart able to pick locks, dismantle expensive Swiss clocks, chase babysitters with car. Chokings from Homer reach 500 milestone.

AGE: 1
Bart's first words are "Ay carumba!" when he catches parents naked in bed one night. Later, father Homer says it was a nightmare. Bart agrees.

AGE: 2
Marge is three months pregnant with Lisa. She recommends leaving small apartment/buying a house. Homer recommends sending Bart to Romanian foreign exchange preschool.

AGE: 2 YEARS, 6 MONTHS
Lisa born. Bart invents activities for himself/new baby sister. Haircuts, glue in diapers, attempted overseas mailings ensue. Perplexed parents seek professional help—watch TV psychiatrist.

AGE: 3
Finally potty-trained, Bart sits on the toilet/ repeatedly states, "I'm a big boy!" Abashed, Homer must now find something new to say when he's on the toilet.

AGE: 5
Bart starts school/has initial positive outlook crushed by heartless teachers. Turns to humor/practical joking for attention. Lifetime of soy milk nose-squirtings begin for best friend Milhouse.

AGE: 10
Bart's 10th year includes: falling down well, Knoxville road trip, credit card fraud, working for Krusty the Clown, insulting entire nation of Australia, and tailbone surgery. Marge says it seems like he's been ten forever.

AGE: 4
Bart performs nightly shadow puppet shows for Lisa, becomes adept at imitating shapes of serpent, devil, goat. Songs of lament and rending of clothing heard from next-door neighbors.

AGE: 6
Bart discovers skateboarding. Simpsons' stairway becomes most dangerous place in the house. Marge takes first-aid correspondence course.

AGE: 9
Bart inexplicably begins rash of wall punchings. Possible cause: family budgetary cutbacks, including switch to non-fluffy toilet paper.

AGE: 3 YEARS, 8 MONTHS
Bart finally warms to Lisa when her first spoken word is "Bart," then helps him raid cookie jar. Noogies, swirlies, Indian burns decrease.

AGE: 7
Bart explores the wonders of spray paint. "El Barto" is born. Signs are altered; police remain baffled.

AGE: 8
Long tradition of staying after school/writing on chalkboard commences. Writes "I'll never earn this punishment again" 100 times.

El Barto

Skinner is a jerk!

I'LL NEVER EARN THIS PUNISHMENT AGAIN
I'LL NEVER EARN THIS PUNISHMENT AGAIN
I'LL NEVER EARN THIS PUNISHMENT AGAIN
I'LL NEVER EARN THIS PUNISHMENT AGAIN
I'LL NEVER EARN THIS PUNISHM
I'LL NEVER EARN THIS PUNISH
I'LL NEVER EARN THIS PUNISH
I'LL NEVER EARN THIS PUNIS
I'LL NEVER EARN THI

LITTLE KNOWN FACT:

Bart's full name is Bartholomew Jojo Simpson. He was born on April 1st, which explains a lot.

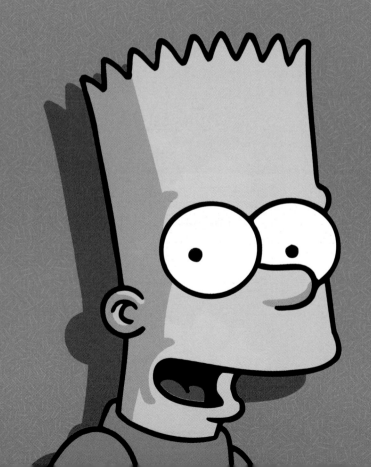

STUFF TO DO
by Bart Simpson

1. Trademark "El Barto."
2. Buy more spray paint.
3. Devise new and interesting ways to make Homer lose it.
4. Find new hiding spot for when Homer loses it.
5. Hide Lisa's saxophone.
6. TiVo "Itchy & Scratchy -a-thon."
7. Think of new catchphrases.
8. Devise new and interesting ways to manipulate Millhouse into doing my dirty work.
9. Practice being more incorrigible.
10. Put off doing homework.
11. Hide Lisa's Malibu Stacy dolls.
12. Get studio audience tickets for Krusty's show.
13. Be first kid in Springfield Elementary cafeteria history to dare to start food fight on Sloppy Joe Day.
14. Work on sass-back.
15. Fine-tune Principal Skinner impersonation.
16. Teach Maggie to spell dirty words with blocks.
17. Hide Lisa's homework.
18. Use the phrase "Blow this Tupperware party" more in conversation.
19. Call Moe's and ask for "G. I. Manidiot."
20. Learn to sleep with eyes open in class.
21. Hide Lisa's Happy Little Elves lunch box.
22. Make a life cast of my butt.
23. Enter butt sculpture in art show at school or make into lamp for Father's Day.
24. Hang out at Kwik-E-Mart.
25. Learn to burp the alphabet.
26. Finish writing underarm symphony
27. "Find" Lisa's missing stuff. Collect reward.
28. Science experiment: Replace parmesan cheese in cafeteria with Groundskeeper Willie's barf-absorbent sawdust. (When kids throw up, will Willie's sawdust be able to absorb itself?)
29. Alter report card.
30. Get little red-haired girl to notice me. (No wait, that's on Charlie Brown's To-Do List.)
31. Convince Milhouse to let me hold his lunch money. Give it to Nelson instead of mine.
32. Publish my memoirs.
33. Pull the fire alarm.
34. Petition to make ice cream the fifth food group.
35. Put mothballs in the beef stew.
36. Hug Mom.

BART ZONES
SCHOOL CAFETERIA

1. Broken air conditioner.
2. Hygiene kit.
3. "Sporks" and the less popular "spifes."
4. V.A. grade beef hearts.
5. Invitation to event of public embarrassment.
6. The Gauntlet.
7. Food depository.
8. Today's Specials.
9. Nutrition dispersal center.
10. Vegetable matter.
11. Foreign matter.
12. ???????
13. Nutrition replenisher.
14. Nutrition converter.
15. Nutritional placement engineer.
16. Forbidden Zone.
17. Bart's handiwork.
18. Highway of lost dental appliances.
19. Milhouse's retainer.
20. Complimentary mints.
21. Politics in action!
22. Bearer of bad news—the school bell ("It tolls for thee").
23. Portals of Doom.
24. Processed, hard, unforgiving, yet strangely comforting, plastic.
25. Food fight ammunition.
26. Food fight instigator.
27. Ralph's lunch.

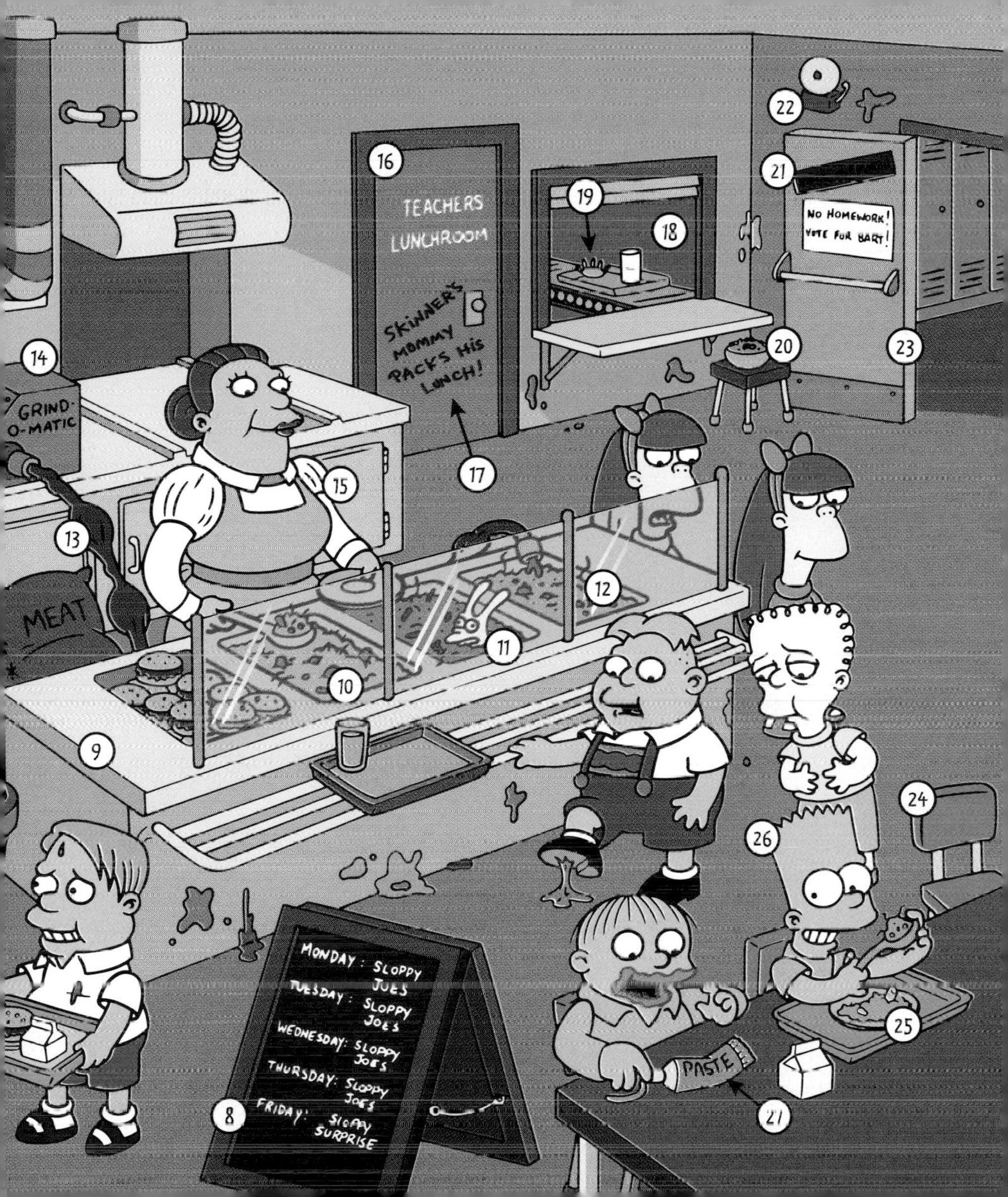

TEACHERS
LUNCHROOM
SKINNER'S MOMMY PACKS HIS LUNCH!
NO HOMEWORK! VOTE FOR BART!
GRIND-O-MATIC
MEAT
MONDAY: SLOPPY JOES
TUESDAY: SLOPPY JOES
WEDNESDAY: SLOPPY JOES
THURSDAY: SLOPPY JOES
FRIDAY: SLOPPY SURPRISE
PASTE
8
9
10
11
12
13
14
15
16
17
18
19
20
21
22
23
24
25
26
27

SEYMOUR SKINNER PRINCIPAL, SPRINGFIELD ELEMENTARY SCHOOL

Principal Skinner holds sway over Springfield Elementary's hallowed halls with an iron fist—if only in his mind. Frequent disciplinary visits to Skinner's office only inspire Bart to immortalize Skinner in rude graffiti by his notorious alter ego, El Barto. Yet, Principal Skinner clings to his dignity by dedicating himself to the most urgent of school challenges: revising and updating the school dress codes, planning the cafeteria lunch menu, and preventing the students from using their imaginations.

Quote: "Ah, 'Diorama-Rama,' my favorite school event next to 'Hearing-Test Thursday.'"

Loves: Fire drills, inflatable bath pillows, antiquing with Mother, and cafeteria Jell-O bricks with grapes in the center.

Member of: MENSA, The Be Sharps, the Springfield NRA, and the Head Lice Awareness Advisory Board.

Nicknames: Spanky and Skinny Boy.

Identifying marks: Metal plate in his butt (got it in 'Nam).

Heart's desire: Edna Krabappel, Bart's 4th grade teacher.

Telltale affliction: Hiccups when upset.

Viet Cong Internment Center Prisoner Number: 24601.

Literary endeavor: Wrote the dinosaur screenplay "Billy and the Clone-O-Saurus."

Trenchant commentary: "The shapely female form has no place in art."

WHAT CAN I SAY? AS A VANDAL AND GRAFFITI ARTIST, PRINCIPAL SKINNER BRINGS OUT THE BEST IN ME.

EDNA KRABAPPEL BART'S 4TH GRADE TEACHER

Divorced and cynical, Edna Krabappel is more than qualified to teach 4th graders—and it shows. She guarantees her classroom conforms to the minimum educational standards mandated by the state—no more, no less. This leaves her free to sneak smokes during educational films, read personal ads during testing times, and slip away on Head Lice Inspection Day for her own private "cootie call" with Principal Skinner.

Quote: "Do what I mean, not what I say."

Secret fear: Bart Simpson will be held back a grade.

Education: Master's Degree in Gothic Psychology from Bryn Mawr.

Fund-raising innovations: Leasing classroom closet space to overcrowded prisons.

Turn-ons: Sailors on shore leave.

Hangout: "Turn Your Head and Coif" Beauty Salon.

Collects: Matchbooks from glamorous nightclubs and green cardigan sweaters.

Hobby: Grinding her teeth, smoking, and hockey.

Favorite snack: Chef Lonely Heart's Soup for One.

Beverage of choice: Chateau Maison Wine on Ice.

Special romantic dessert: Applesauce.

LOVE REALLY CHANGES YOU. WHEN MRS. KRABAPPEL AND PRINCIPAL SKINNER GOT TOGETHER, I WENT FROM A GOOD-FOR-NOTHING TO A GO-BETWEEN IN JUST SECONDS.

MARTIN PRINCE BART'S GENIUS CLASSMATE

Lute playing, tattle-telling, teacher's pet Martin Prince is the smartest kid in Bart's class and the quintessential nerd. Though he taught Bart the importance of adequate plant life to a study area in return for the secrets of slingshots and graffiti, he remains a constant irritant—on one occasion successfully lobbying to have the school day extended twenty minutes.

Quote: "The preferred spelling of wiener is "W-I-E-N-E-R" although E-I is an acceptable ethnic variant."

I.Q.: 216.

Celebrity impersonations: Ernest Hemingway, Phileas Fogg, Julia Child.

Martin's helpful hints: Put a pinch of sage in your boots and all day long a spicy scent is your reward.

Favorite magazine: Junior Skeptic.

Favorite video game: My Dinner with André.

Martin's "Did You Know?": The common box-kite was originally used as a means of drying wet string.

Shirt pocket: Never without a pen.

Number of swim trunks worn to avoid being pantsed: 17.

Pets: A Shar-pei, a guinea pig, and an asparagus fern named Copernicus.

IT'S GUYS LIKE MARTIN WHO MAKE THE REST OF US FEEL NORMAL.

From the matching bows in their hair to their lovely color coordinated frocks and shoes, Sherri and Terri dress alike. They walk, talk and mock alike. Sweetness and light on the outside, they delight in the misfortune of others, especially Bart, and do what they can to help it along. They love tormenting people by answering to each other's name. In fact, they have done this so often that even they are not sure which is which.

Quote: (Double word balloon) "I'm Sherri. She's Terri."

Nicknames: Terri and Sherri.

Secret desire: To be united in one body.

Secret fear: It might be too crowded in there.

Extra-curricular activities: Studying tap with Little Vicki Valentine, playing piccolo in the Springfield Elementary Band, repeatedly calling the Corey Hotline and hanging up.

Favorite games: Truth or Dare, Marco Polo, making faces at people behind their backs.

In the event of nuclear disaster: The fallout shelter has space for Sherri, but not Terri.

YOU DON'T WANT TO GET THEM ON YOUR BAD SIDE. THEY'LL SURROUND YOU.

Though frequently involved in random collisions, Otto remains true to the Bus Driver's Pledge: "Never crash the bus on purpose." He relates well to Bart, having spent three years in the 4th grade himself. They both share a fondness for comic books, heavy metal, and "sticking it to the man"—and neither sees much point in bathing

Quote: "My name is Ot-to! I'm hot to trot-o!"

Identifying marks: Big Daddy Roth tattoo on butt.

Leisure pursuits: Snowboarding, bungee jumping, acid flashbacks.

Favorite music: Led Zeppelin, Black Sabbath's "Iron Man," Edgar Winters' "Frankenstein," and the soothing compilation "Songs to Enrage Bus Drivers."

Special skills: Air guitar, carnival Rocket Car ride operator, can fake his own death.

Heavy metal bands kicked out of: The Screechies, Dopey, The Unemployed, and Büssdryver.

Proud driving record: Fifteen crashes without a single fatality.

Otto's creed: A bus driver is truck-worthy, laid-back, healthful, surly, flirtatious, speedy, cool, raving, keen, and irreverent.

Pedigree: Father is an admiral; Mother is ashamed.

OTTO'S GOT IT MADE. HE DRIVES TO SPRINGFIELD ELEMENTARY EVERY DAY, BUT HE NEVER HAS TO GO INSIDE.

GROUNDSKEEPER WILLIE HEAD GROUNDSKEEPER, SPRINGFIELD ELEMENTARY

Conceived, born, and educated on a pool table in a tavern near Loch Ness, Groundskeeper Willie is an irascible shaggy-haired Scotsman with a huge reservoir of pent-up rage, which he vents constantly. At the faintest sign of trouble, he rips off his shirt and hurls his rippling muscular body into action. Despite an inability to wrangle a second date from anyone, Willie won't give up on romance—spending most of his free time videotaping couples in the privacy of their cars.

Quote: "Ach, yer nothin' but a bath-takin', underpants-wearin' lily-hugger!"

Secret shame: Father was hung for stealing a pig.

Claim to fame: Stole seven pigs in one night.

Turn-ons: Grease, wearing kilts, wrestling wolves, and Chewbacca.

Turn-offs: Cheese-eating surrender monkeys, creamed corn, and people who wear underwear.

Prized possession: His shovel, "Agnes."

Alternate profession: Substitute French teacher.

His secret obsession: British nanny Shary Bobbins.

Failed culinary venture: Chef Willie's Haggis Helper.

Musical accomplishments: An album of traditional Scottish pig-stealing songs entitled "Papa's Got a Brand-New Bagpipe."

Future plans: To build a security bog around his prize-winning heather, catch a leprechaun, and marry his tractor.

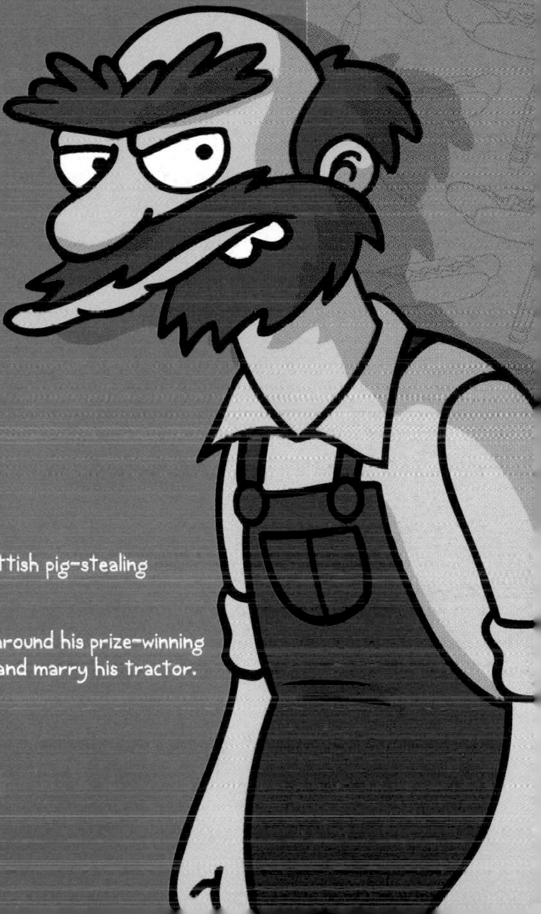

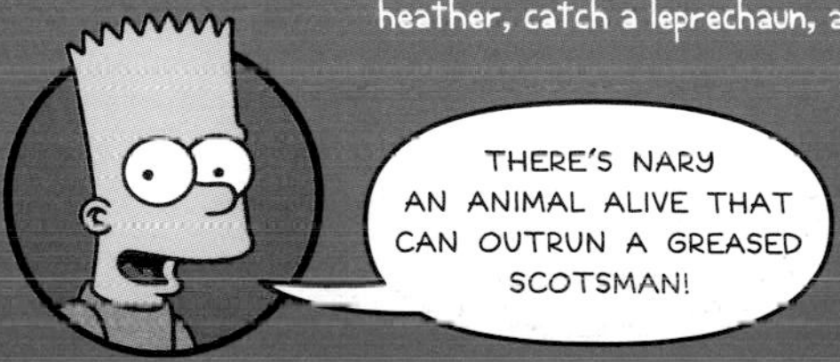
THERE'S NARY AN ANIMAL ALIVE THAT CAN OUTRUN A GREASED SCOTSMAN!

BART'S PULLABLE PRANKS

During the day, change all the lightbulbs in your house from normal to colored. At night, watch the fun!

NOTEWORTHY FUN

Pass a note you know will be intercepted by the teacher. The note says something like "Isn't learning a wonderful thing?" or "My, the teacher looks particularly beautiful today!"

SCHOOL SURVIVAL
HANDBOOK

 WARNING!
DO NOT LET THIS FALL INTO
THE HANDS OF TEACHERS,
PRINCIPALS, OR OTHER
HUMORLESS AUTHORITY FIGURES!

TURN THE PAGE IF YOU DARE, MAN!

CLASSROOM TACTICS

THE SEATING CHART:
Gaining the high ground in the class struggle

FRONT ROW
NERDS, GOODY-GOODIES, AND OVER-ACHIEVERS

THE SNITCH
NEED WE SAY MORE?

DANGER ZONE
SHADED AREAS SUBJECT TO MAXIMUM TEACHER SCRUTINY

BEST SEAT IN THE HOUSE
LOCATION, LOCATION, LOCATION.

MORONS IN THE BACK ROW
PERSIST IN MISGUIDED BELIEF THAT THEY ARE INVISIBLE

THE BRAINIAC
A NEARBY SEAT IS A BIG PLUS AT EXAM TIME

WHATSISNAME
NEVER SPEAKS UP, NEVER ACTS UP—WHO IS HE, ANYWAY?

THE PERKY GIRL
ACTUALLY SEEMS TO BE ENJOYING HERSELF

THE MALCONTENT
IS THIS YOU?

THE SMUG ONES
20 YEARS FROM NOW, THEY'LL STILL BE A SOURCE OF IRRITATION

BE CAREFUL:

WITH TEACHERS:
NEVER MAKE DIRECT EYE CONTACT

WITH REPORTS:
KEEP IT VAGUE AND UNOPINIONATED

WITH CAFETERIA FOOD: MAY CAUSE UNKNOWN SIDE EFFECTS

IF YOU ARE CAUGHT DOING ANYTHING:

- ACT SHOCKED, SPEECHLESS, AND HURT (THIS WILL BUY YOU TIME TO THINK UP A BETTER EXCUSE).
- TRY THE OLD RELIABLE: "IDIDN'TDOITNOBODYSAWME-DOITYOUCAN'TPROVEANYTHING."
- CONFESS IMMEDIATELY—THIS WILL CONFUSE AND UNBALANCE YOUR OPPONENT.

TRY THIS EXTRA-CREDIT BRAIN TEASER!

Q: Is school a valuable opportunity for intellectual stimulation and growth, or just a way to get you out of your parents' hair for 12 years?

A: Yes.

GUERILLA STRATEGIES

HERE ARE SEVERAL FIELD-TESTED WAYS TO COPE WITH THIS WEIRD TEMPORAL PHENOMENON:

DOODLE
EASY, FUN, AND ARTISTICALLY SATISFYING. ADDED BENEFIT: TEACHER MAY ACTUALLY THINK YOU ARE WORKING

USE SIGN LANGUAGE
HINT: WORKS BEST WHEN TEACHER'S BACK IS TURNED

PASS NOTES
CAUTION: ALTHOUGH IT MAY LOOK COOL IN OLD MOVIES, SWALLOWING A NOTE WHEN CAUGHT IS PROBABLY NOT A GOOD IDEA

GO TO THE RESTROOM
10 (MINUTES PER TRIP) X 6 (CLASSES PER DAY) =
25 FEWER DAYS OF CLASS PER YEAR

WHEN ALL ELSE FAILS
LISTEN TO THE TEACHER—
YOU COULD POSSIBLY LEARN
SOMETHING INTERESTING

THINGS TEACHERS DON'T WANT TO HEAR WHEN THEY SAY, "ARE THERE ANY QUESTIONS?"

"May I go to the bathroom?"   "Will this be on the test?"
"Could you repeat that?"   "Was that A.D. or B.C.?"

Know Your Enemy:
THE TEACHER
Ticking Time Bomb of the Classroom

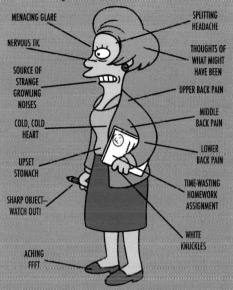

MENACING GLARE

NERVOUS TIC

SOURCE OF STRANGE GROWLING NOISES

COLD, COLD HEART

UPSET STOMACH

SHARP OBJECT— WATCH OUT!

ACHING FEET

SPLITTING HEADACHE

THOUGHTS OF WHAT MIGHT HAVE BEEN

UPPER BACK PAIN

MIDDLE BACK PAIN

LOWER BACK PAIN

TIME-WASTING HOMEWORK ASSIGNMENT

WHITE KNUCKLES

REMEMBER: YOU WILL EVENTUALLY GRADUATE* AND GET OUT OF THIS PLACE, BUT YOUR TEACHER IS STUCK
HERE PERMANENTLY. (THIS MAY EXPLAIN WHY HE OR SHE GETS A MITE TESTY AT TIMES.)
*BE SURE YOU DO

WHAT DOES MY FUTURE HOLD?

AND IF YOU DO SURVIVE SCHOOL, THEN WHAT? HERE'S ONE WAY TO FIND OUT!

A SIMPLE QUIZ
NO STUDYING
NO CHEATING

1. When you are picked on by the school bully, do you:
   A. Tell the principal?
   B. Tell the teacher?
   C. Hide in your locker?
   D. Attempt to distract him with witty repartee?

2. When the teacher asks if you have your homework, do you:
   A. Say: "Yes, ma'am, and I'd like to say that I found the subject quite fascinating and stimulating."?
   B. Say: "The dog ate it."?
   C. Say: "Homework? What homework?"
   D. Attempt to distract her with witty repartee?

3. When called upon to read your book report, do you:
   A. Deliver a stirring account of Lee Iacocca's autobiography?
   B. Give a competent synopsis of Black Beauty?
   C. Summarize the latest issue of Radioactive Man?
   D. Bluff your way through Treasure Island?

SCORING
Count 4 points for each A answer, 3 for each B, 2 for each C, and 1 for each D. Now find your point total in the list below to discover your future career:

12 POINTS Politician, media figure, corporate executive, school principal.

9–11 POINTS Mid-level bureaucrat, IRS agent, schoolteacher

4–8 POINTS Assistant manager of fast food franchise, car salesman, vice-president of the United States

0–3 POINTS Publishers' Clearinghouse sweepstakes entrant, daytime TV viewer, embittered struggling artist

---

FIGHTING BACK
A THREE-STEP APPROACH

1. TAKE CAREFUL NOTES ON ALL THE BORING, STUPID, AND UNFAIR THINGS GOING ON AROUND YOU
2. WAIT 20 YEARS
3. USE NOTES AS BASIS FOR WILDLY SUCCESSFUL TV SERIES

EXCUSES, EXCUSES

FALLBACK PLOYS IN CASE OF CAPTURE

VERBAL MANEUVERING

(NOTE: IN FACE-TO-FACE CONFRONTATIONS, ATTITUDE IS KEY; MEMORIZE THE FOLLOWING SO YOU CAN RESPOND TO CHALLENGES QUICKLY & CONFIDENTLY.)

FOR ADVANCED STUDENTS:

THE FORGED NOTE

STRUCTURE THE CONTENTS TO ALLAY SUSPICIONS ABOUT ITS AUTHENTICITY.

DEAR MRS. KRABAPPEL,

PLEASE EXCUSE BART'S ABSENCE YESTERDAY. HE WAS SICK.

Marge Simpson

P.S. I AM DICTATING THIS NOTE TO BART BECAUSE MY EYES ARE HEAVILY BANDAGED DUE TO A FREAK KITCHEN ACCIDENT. HOWEVER, I'M SURE I'LL BE FULLY RECOVERED BY THE NEXT TIME I SEE YOU AND WILL NOT WISH TO BE REMINDED OF THIS GRUESOME INCIDENT.

REMEMBER THE 3 "P"s

PROPER EXECUTION REQUIRES **PRE-PLANNING, PRACTICE,** AND **PREPARATION.**

SO YOU'RE LA

DEALING WITH THE SYSTEM'S INABILITY TO

SNEAKING INTO CLASS:
MASTER THESE FOUR FIELD-TESTED TECHN

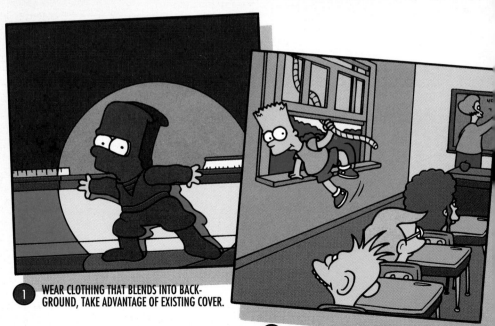

1. WEAR CLOTHING THAT BLENDS INTO BACK-GROUND, TAKE ADVANTAGE OF EXISTING COVER.

2. USE AN ALTERNATE ENTRANCE.

TE-SO WHAT?

COMPREHEND THIS UTTERLY NATURAL BEHAVIOR

A BEGINNER'S GUIDE
QUES AND FEAR DETENTION NO MORE!

4. HAVE YOUR FRIENDS CREATE A DIVERSION.

3. CRAWL TO YOUR SEAT,
LET YOUR HEAD RISE SLOWLY INTO VIEW.

BACK TO SCHOOL

GATHERING THE SEEDS OF WISDOM TO PREPARE FOR THE LEAN MONTHS AHEAD

FACT!

HUMANS ARE THE ONLY ANIMALS THAT ATTEND SCHOOL

LEARN FROM NATURE

SCHOOL AVOIDANCE TECHNIQUES ADAPTED FROM THE ANIMAL KINGDOM

MIGRATION
TRAVEL TO MORE HOSPITABLE ENVIRONMENT, PREFERABLY BEYOND THE JURISDICTION OF LOCAL TRUANT AUTHORITIES

HIBERNATION
WITH THE PROPER ATITUDE AND PLENTY OF LATE-NIGHT TV, YOU CAN SLEEP THROUGH ALMOST ANYTHING

THE FIRST DAY
"THAT WHICH DOES NOT DESTROY ME MAKES ME STRONGER." —FRIEDRICH NIETZSCHE

DO NOT DELAY! THE PRESTIGIOUS TITLE "CLASS CLOWN" IS OFTEN AWARDED IN THE FORMATIVE FIRST WEEK OF SCHOOL.

REMEMBER: BUILD UP YOUR RESISTANCE! LIKE ALL TOXIC SUBSTANCES, CAFETERIA FOOD REQUIRES AN ADJUSTMENT PERIOD. START WITH SMALL DOSES AND WORK GRADUALLY TOWARD A COMPLETE MEAL.

WHEN THINGS LOOK BLEAKEST: BE GRATEFUL YOU'RE NOT THE NEW KID.

PREPARATION=SUCCESS

Fine-tuned, the right notebook becomes a powerful tool:

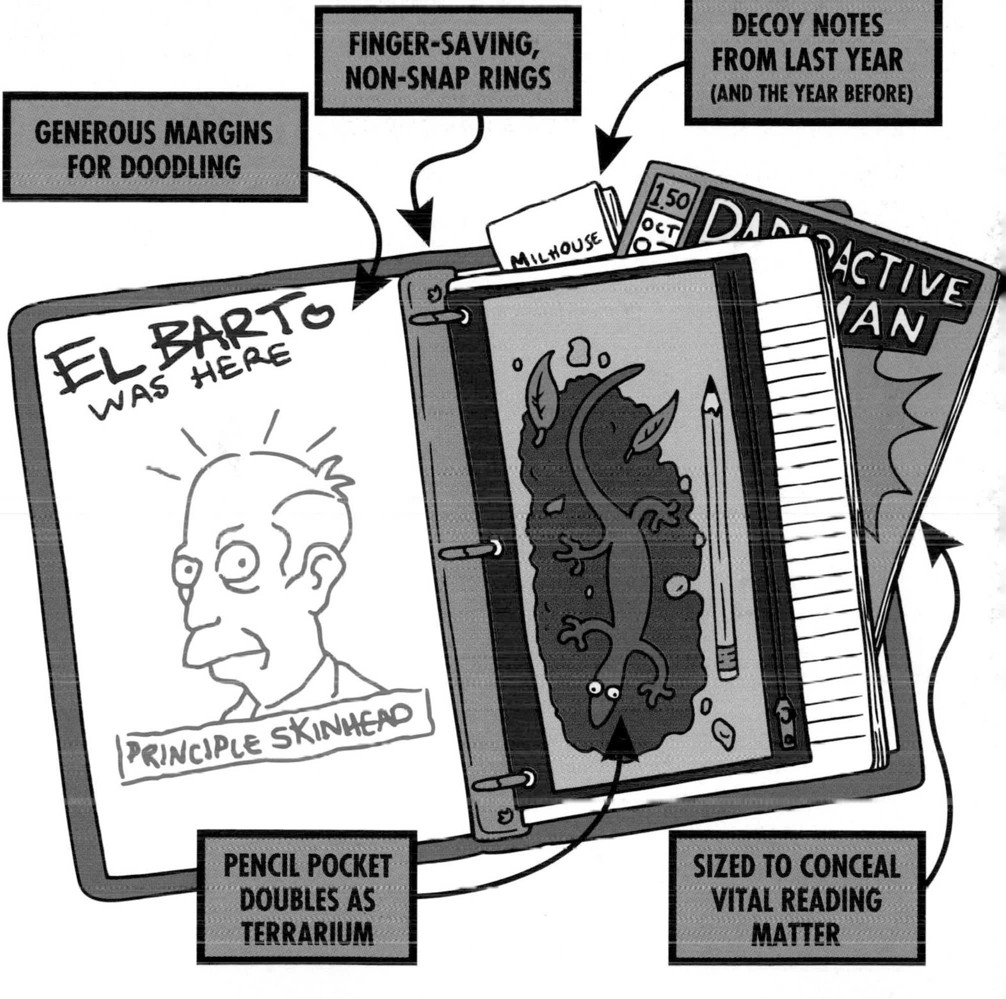
FINGER-SAVING, NON-SNAP RINGS
DECOY NOTES FROM LAST YEAR (AND THE YEAR BEFORE)
GENEROUS MARGINS FOR DOODLING
MILHOUSE
1.50
OCT
EL BARTO WAS HERE
PRINCIPLE SKINHEAD
PENCIL POCKET DOUBLES AS TERRARIUM
SIZED TO CONCEAL VITAL READING MATTER

BACK ON THE

THE SOFTY
LOOK FOR: Use of smiley-face stickers.
PROS: Lets you get away with a lot.
CONS: Will draw the line eventually.
ADVICE: Beware of major backlash if pushed too far.

THE WANNABE HIPSTER
LOOK FOR: No Doubt T-shirt.
PROS: Watches MTV.
CONS: Thinks watching MTV makes him really cool.
ADVICE: Wait until his back is turned to laugh at him.

CHAIN GANG

YET ANOTHER SCHOOL YEAR
NEW TEACHER
DETERMINING YOUR STRATEGY FOR THE REST OF THE YEAR

THE LAME DUCK
LOOK FOR: Weary, resigned facade; merciless heart.
PROS: With only two years until retirement,
he's thrown in the towel.
CONS: Has heard it all before.
ADVICE: Warning: true nature revealed at grade time.

THE DOMINATRIX
 LOOK FOR: Pent-up fury.
PROS: None.
CONS: Too many to list.
ADVICE: Transfer!

KEEP YOUR FRI
YOUR ENEM

IDENTIFY YOUR
UNDERSTAND THE CLASSROOM POWER

THE BULLY

LOOK FOR: Bruised knuckles.

PROS: Draws teacher's fire away from you.

CONS: May pay you back later.

ADVICE: Don't let him catch you alone; he travels in packs, so you should too.

THE EGGHEAD

LOOK FOR: Self-satisfied smirk.

PROS: Knows all the answers.

CONS: Probably won't tell them to you.

ADVICE: Maintain good relations, especially near exam time.

NEW CLASSMATES
STRUCTURE AND MAKE IT WORK FOR YOU

THE TATTLETALE

LOOK FOR: Shifty eyes, nervous twitch.
PROS: Can be deployed to your advantage.
CONS: No loyalty whatsoever.
ADVICE: Sit as far away from her as possible.

THE CRYBABY

LOOK FOR: Snot on shirt sleeve.
PROS: Easy target.
CONS: Can turn into "The Tattletale."
ADVICE: Make sure there are no witnesses.

THE SCHOOL BUS

1. ***THE BUS DRIVER*** - You can't sit here.
2. ***SMUG SAFETY PATROLLERS*** - They sit at the front so no one can avoid their contemptuous gaze.
3. ***THE NAUSEOUS KID*** - Usually sits in the middle of bus where jostling is minimal. Stay clear.
4. ***THE INDIFFERENTS*** - These kids really don't care where they sit. Which is why they always end up sitting in the same exact spot.
5. ***THE AUDIENCE*** - For people who enjoy the spectacle coming from the back of the bus but don't want the stigma of actually sitting back there.
6. ***REBELS WITHOUT A CAR*** - Back here you can horse around with impunity or just relax in a pulsating massage of potholes and speed bumps.

DEALING WITH THE INEVITABLE "HOW I SPENT MY SUMMER VACATION" REPORT

Assigning summer vacation stories is an easy out for teachers who haven't gotten their act together by the first days of school. Let's face it: They really don't care what you did, they're just trying to figure out what to do with you. So spice up their life if they're paying attention, and entertain the class if they're not. These stories usually come down to a case of one-upsmanship anyway, so go for broke. Make up something cool. For example, other students probably visited their grandmothers over the summer, but did they visit her... in prison!? Sure, a few people went to camp. But was their counselor Osama Bin Laden in disguise? Take your everyday stories and elaborate. Your classmates will thank you.

INVALUABLE FASHION TIP

Never, ever, let your mom go shopping for clothes without your direct supervision. Face it, by avoiding responsibility now, you're only setting yourself up for ridicule later.

If all else fails and your mom forces you to go to school looking like a geek, wear a T-shirt featuring the authority-baiting icon of your choice under your mom-approved outfit. Once you get to school, stash the geek clothes in your locker. (Hint: Remember to change back before you go home.)

ET'S-LAY IT-SPLAY O-TAY THE EACH-BAY!

SECRET
for the

CAN YOU BELIEVE THIS DRIVEL?
(Move finger up and down on upper lip)

AY CARUMBA!

CHECK OUT THE HAIR ON THAT ONE!
(Tug on hair in front)

I LIKE HIM / HER

ARE WE THE ONLY ONES WHO SEE THE ABSURDITY OF THIS?
(Spin hands in circles)

I LOATHE HIM / HER

SHOW ME YOUR ANSWERS
(Twirl pencil in direction of friend)

CHECK OUT THAT OUTFIT!
(Tug on collar)

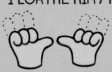

I'M GOING TO HAVE A CONNIPTION IF THEY DON'T STOP TALKING
(Move fingers up and down)

CODES
classroom

MY THOUGHTS EXACTLY!

GET ME OUT OF THIS SITUATION NOW!
(Tug on ear)

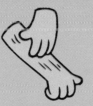
WHAT A GEEK!
(Brush fingers down arm)

LET'S GO MAN!
(With palm down, rub thumb up and down)

LET'S STAY
(Hold palm up)

THEY'RE CRAZY!
(Scratch alternate arms 3 times)

DON'T SAY ONE MORE WORD, OR I WILL DIE AND THEN KILL YOU!
(Fingers locked, snap heels of palms back and forth)

WHAT AN AIRHEAD!
(Pull invisible string through ears back and forth)

EW! B.O. ALERT!

PRESENTING THE
THE SKATEBOARD OF

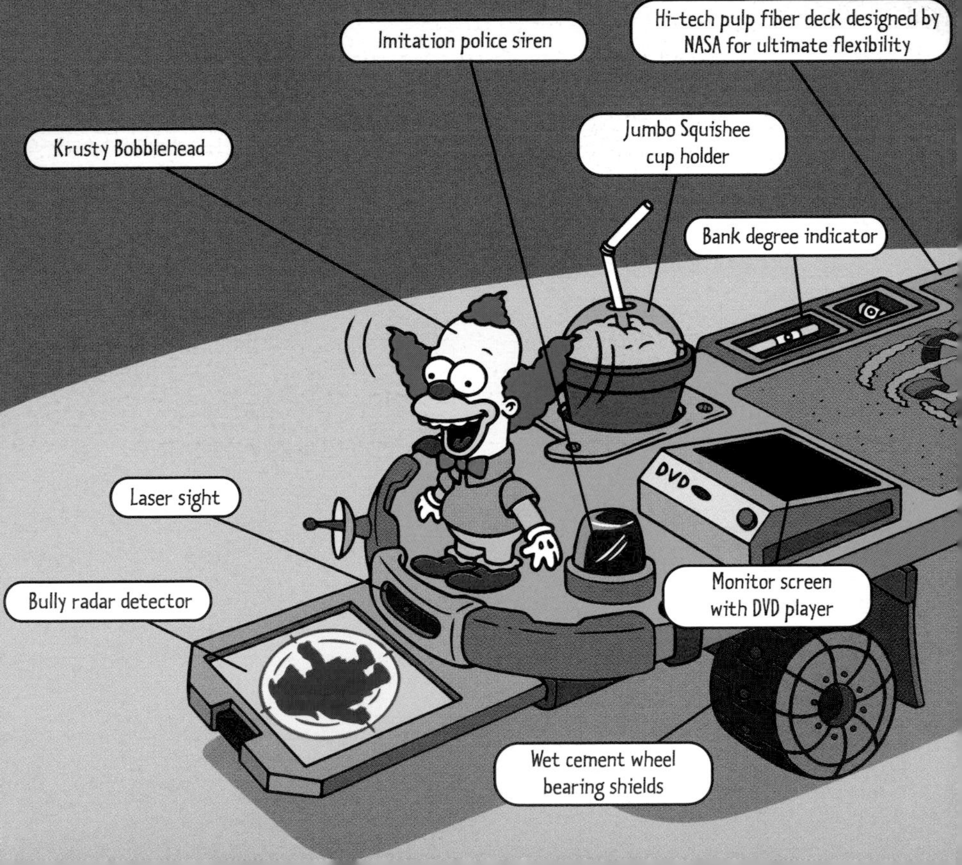
Hi-tech pulp fiber deck designed by NASA for ultimate flexibility
Imitation police siren
Krusty Bobblehead
Jumbo Squishee cup holder
Bank degree indicator
DVD
Laser sight
Bully radar detector
Monitor screen with DVD player
Wet cement wheel bearing shields

BARTFINK
BART'S DREAMS

Graphic by "Tommy the Needle,"
Ethnic Town's premier tattoo artist

English to Thrasher
Dictionary

Emergency parachute
deployment array.

Flesh rending grip tape

Not pictured:
(underside of board)

- Oil slick discharge tank.
- Grind spark suppresser.
- Automatic-lift truck suspension.
- Global positioning satellite chip.
- Spring-loaded kick turn piston.
- Nose slide Teflon coating.
- First aid kit for face plant wipeouts.

Detachable windsheer fins

Retractable wheel spikes

Backside grab rail

Mini mudflaps

MUTANT

ALL TOGETHER NOW! A **ONE**, AND A **TWO**, AND A...

WE HAVE NO SCHOOL TODAY
(to the tune of "Ta-Ra-Ra-Boom-Dee-Ay")

We have no school today! It is some holiday!
I don't know which, per se.
But who cares, anyway?!

SHOW & TELL
(to the tune of "Jingle Bells")

Show and Tell! Show and Tell!
Objects on display.
Oh, how dull it is to see
your Grandpa's old toupee-ee!

Show and Tell! Show and Tell!
Ashtrays made of clay.
A rusty crank from a broken bank
and a fat pet cat named Ray.

One day Nelson Muntz
brought in a bee hive,
opened it to find
the bees were still alive! (Ow, ow, ow!)

Spoiled Martin Prince
showed off his Monet.
When it slipped and ripped in two
he cried and ran away!

Oh...
Show and Tell! Show and Tell!
(etc., repeat ad nauseam)

MELODIES

THE BATTLE HYMN OF THE BLACKBOARD

(to the tune of "The Battle Hymn of the Republic")

My hands were on the gradebook where the students' marks are stored.
The teacher burst upon the scene.
"Put down that book!" she roared.
Now I'm writing out these words one hundred times on the blackboard:
"I will not steal gradebooks."

Man, this task is disconcertin'.
Ow, my writing hand is hurtin'.
There is one thing that is certain:
I will not steal gradebooks.

I'VE BEEN WORKING ON MY HOMEWORK

(to the tune of "I've Been Working on the Railroad")

I've been working on my homework, while I watch TV.
I've been working on my homework, while I skateboard down the street.
Can't you hear the teacher calling,
"Your book report is due!"
"Here it is," I calmly answer, "All in one sentence, too."
"Here's my book report, here's my book report for you-ou-ou
"Here's my book report, here's my book report,
All in one sentence, too."

THE SUPER-STRETCH WAISTBAND

(to the tune of "The Star-Spangled Banner")

Oh, say, can you see,
through the trees over there,
what so proudly we pulled
up the flagpole last Friday,
from the locker room grabbed,
leaving someone's butt bare,
when we fed the flag rope
through the
brand name tag sideways?

Up there blowing around,
a stretch waistband its crown,
you would think that by now,
they'd have taken it down.

Oh, say, does that underwear
still flap in the breeze,
o'er the classrooms, the schoolyard,
the parking lot and the trees?!

Annoy, Annoy, Annoy, Your Teacher

(to the tune of "Row, Row, Row, Your Boat")

Annoy, annoy, annoy your teacher
By yelling her first name.
Emily! Emily! Emily! Emily!
You'll drive her insane.

BART'S RECIPES FOR

#12 - THE FAST FOOD AND THE FURIOUS

1. Call a fast food joint that sells chicken fingers.
2. Ask the unsuspecting minimum wage slave on the other end of the phone, "Do you have chicken fingers?"
3. When they answer "yes" say, "Well, it must hurt when you pick your nose!"
4. Laugh like a maniac and hang up.

TELEPHONE FUN

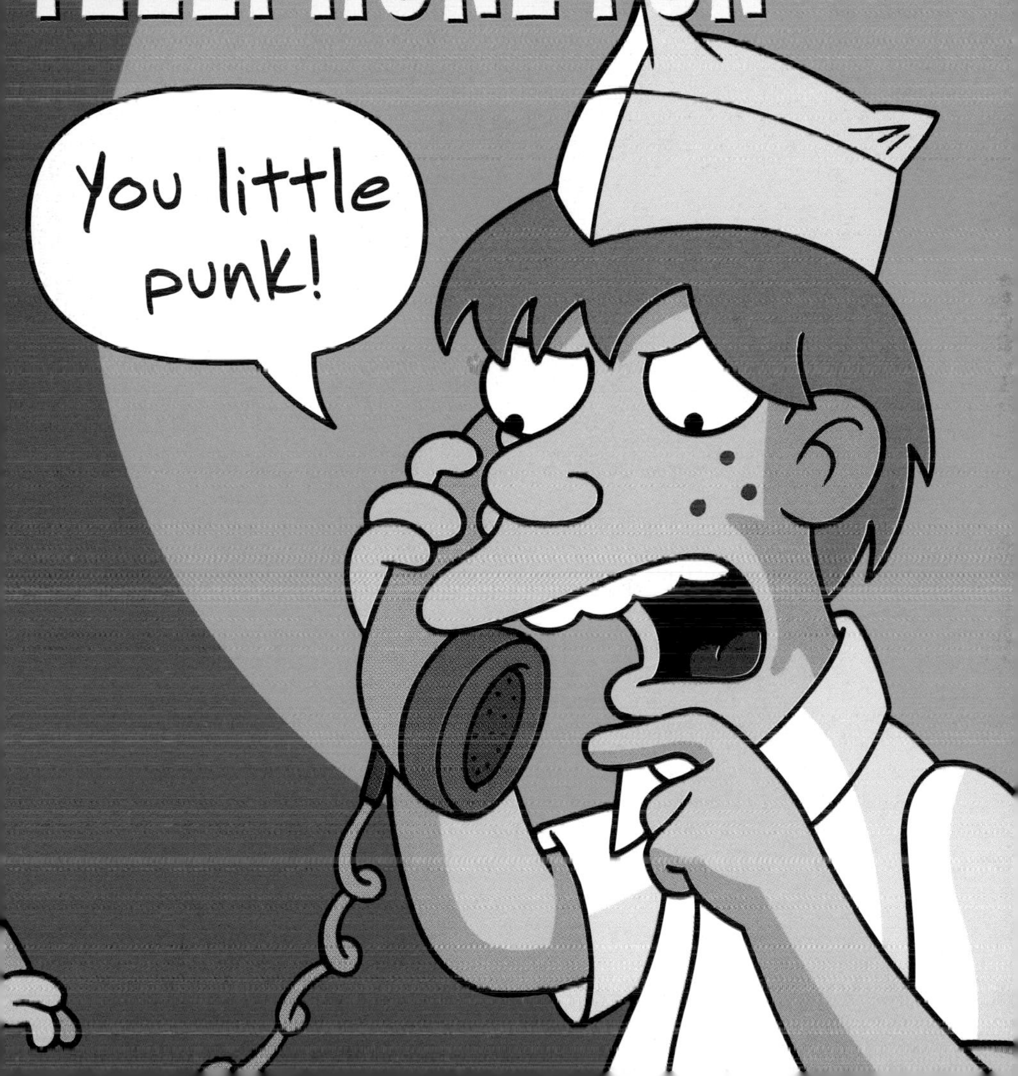
You little punk!

THE ANATOMY OF BART

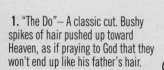

1. "The Do"— A classic cut. Bushy spikes of hair pushed up toward Heaven, as if praying to God that they won't end up like his father's hair.

2. Hard Drive — Above average, but function is often impaired by Squishee brain freezes, television, and mind-rotting comic books.

3. Nose — For trouble.

4. Ears — Selectively able to tune out all requests to do homework, clean room, take out garbage, "act more like your sister," etc.

5. Trap — A finely tuned insult machine; ground zero for numerous popular catchphrases.

6. Neck— Oft-rung target of Homer's frustration.

7. Skateboard — For transportation to and from school; also a tried and true method for quick getaways.

8. Pockets — Where detention slips go to die.

9. Reading Material — Classroom distraction that fits well inside most textbooks.

10. Guns - Future site of dangerous-looking tattoos.

11. Booty — Displayed au naturel on a regular basis, often in public places and aimed at authority figures, such as Principal Skinner, Mayor Quimby, and Mr. Burns.

12. Legs — Flexible for shredding. Fast for running "from the man." Remarkably fatigued when there is work to be done.

13. Feet— Counting the minutes till that first barefoot day of summer.

WHAT'S ON BART'S MIND?

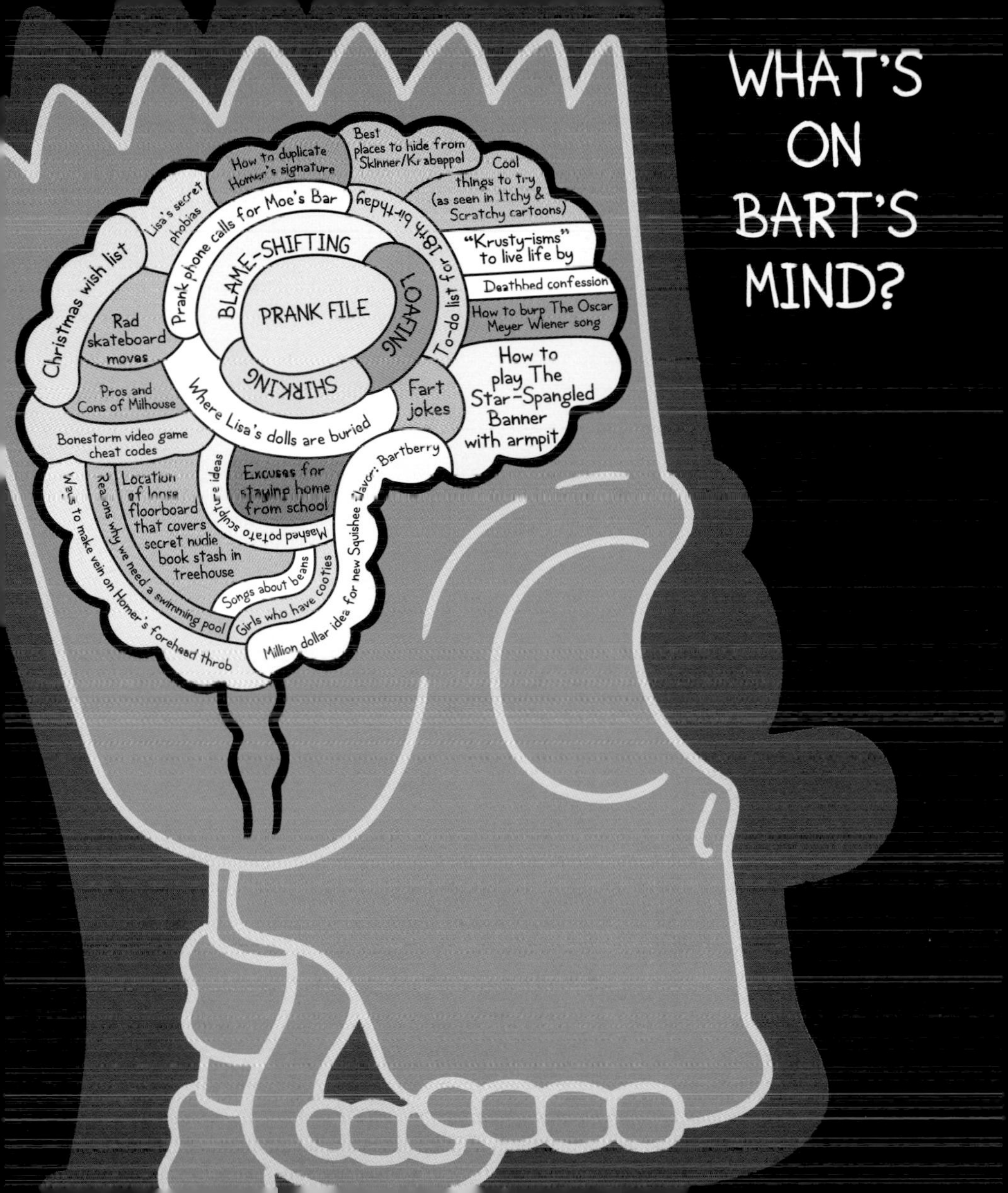

PRANK FILE
BLAME-SHIFTING
LOAFING
SHIRKING
Prank phone calls for Moe's Bar
To-do list for 18th birthday
Where Lisa's dolls are buried
How to duplicate Homer's signature
Best places to hide from Skinner/Krabappel
Cool things to try (as seen in Itchy & Scratchy cartoons)
"Krusty-isms" to live life by
Deathbed confession
How to burp The Oscar Meyer Wiener song
How to play The Star-Spangled Banner with armpit
Fart jokes
Lisa's secret phobias
Christmas wish list
Rad skateboard moves
Pros and Cons of Milhouse
Bonestorm video game cheat codes
Excuses for staying home from school
Mashed potato sculpture ideas
Location of loose floorboard that covers secret nudie book stash in treehouse
Reasons why we need a swimming pool
Ways to make vein on Homer's forehead throb
Songs about beans
Girls who have cooties
Million dollar idea for new Squishee flavor: Bartberry

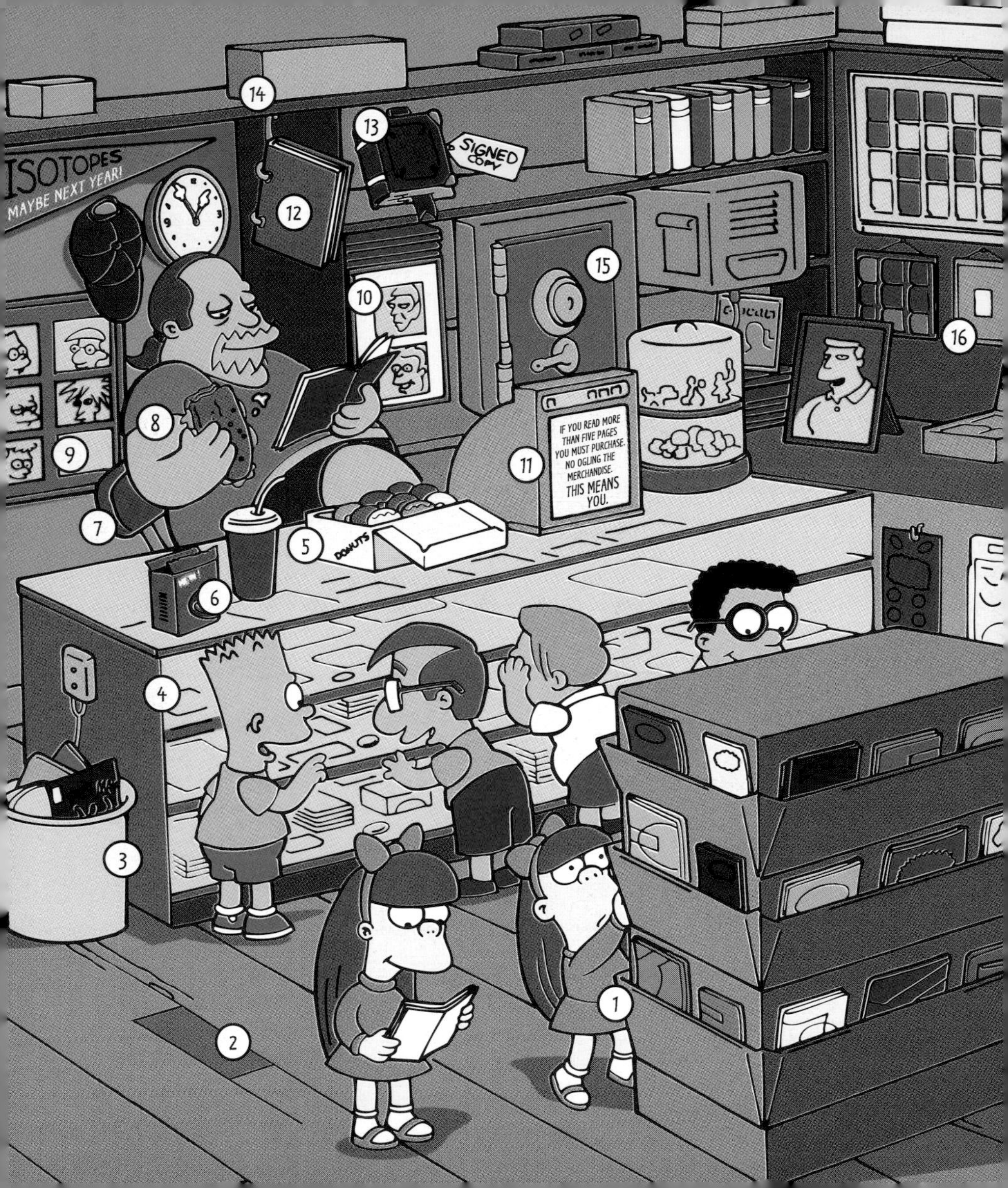
ISOTOPES
MAYBE NEXT YEAR!
SIGNED COPY
IF YOU READ MORE THAN FIVE PAGES YOU MUST PURCHASE. NO OGLING THE MERCHANDISE. THIS MEANS YOU.
DONUTS
1
2
3
4
5
6
7
8
9
10
11
12
13
14
15
16

BART ZONES
ANDROID'S DUNGEON

1. Girl's section (Malibu Stacey comics, Happy Little Elves, E–Z Bake Oven Tales).
2. Honus Wagner card (underneath floorboards)—even the Comic Book Guy doesn't know this is here.
3. Trash (filled with "Biclops" comics).
4. Case of Extreme Value—"For serious buyers only!" (Features Radioactive Man #45 "Fallout with Fallout," "Itchy & Scratchy" original animation cel, John F. Kennedy's favorite nickel and Luis Gonzalez's chewing gum.)
5. Breakfast, lunch, and dinner.
6. Snacks—box of marshmallow peeps.
7. Throne—never moved, rarely lonely.
8. Owner, Proprietor & Dictator—Comic Book Guy.
9. Banned for Life Gallery.
10. Always Welcome Wall (Nimoy & Shatner).
11. Cash Register—Also a collector's item.
12. The Store's Bible (Comics Price Guide).
13. The Real Bible.
14. Batman creator Bob Kane's mummified drawing hand.
15. Top Secret Bootleg Video Vault. (Titles include: "Mr. Rogers Drunk," and "The 2nd Zapruder Film.")
16. Rare 1973 Carl Yastrzemski "Mutton Chops" baseball card.
17. Krusty Kards ("Collect all 10,000. Hurry, my bookie's getting ornery!")
18. Radio (for listening to Art Bell only).
19. Fortress of Solitude (Bathroom).

COMIC BOOK GUY OWNER OF THE ANDROID'S DUNGEON & BASEBALL CARD SHOP

Sarcastic, surly, insulting, and rude, Comic Book Guy is the master of his domain, disdainful to all. Even when customers pay good money for his overpriced collectibles, he treats them like children. Except for the children, he treats them like babies. Forty-five and friendless, Comic Book Guy maintains his bovine good looks by rigorously studying the world's great dietary regimens—then ignoring them.

Quote: "Make like my pants and split."

Store motto: Take me to your Comic Books and Baseball Cards.

Thumbs-up: The Green Lantern, Thundra, Ghost Rider, Xena, Doctor Who, and Zebra Girl.

Thumbs-down: Superman.

Education: Masters Degree in Folklore and Mythology.

Rival store: Frodo's of Shelbyville.

Ultimate fantasy: An hour on the holodeck with Seven-of-Nine.

Selected bumper stickers: "My Other Car Is a Millenium Falcon," "I Brake for Tribbles," "Keep Honking, I'm Charging My Phaser," and "Kang is My Co-Pilot."

Favorite foods: Marshmallow peeps, malted-milk balls, confectioners' sugar, chocolate frosting, and tacos.

His final frontier: Human contact.

WHAT A LIFE! HE'S LIVING EVERY KID'S DREAM, EXCEPT THAT HE'S AN ADULT.

RADIOACTIVE MAN & FALLOUT BOY COSTUMED SUPER HEROES

Filthy rich playboy Claude Kane III becomes Radioactive Man after being caught in a test explosion of the top-secret Mega-Bomb. His ward, Rod Runtledge, gains his superpowers through a freak accident during a high-school science experiment. Together, these Champions of Justice defend Americanism, fight nonconformists and make the world safe for rampant consumerism.

Quote: (Radioactive Man) "Up and Atom!" (Fallout Boy) "Jiminy Jillickers!"

Greatest foe: Doctor Crab, who has the proportionate strength and cunning of a large crab.

Other villains: Hypno Head, Larceny Lass, Brain-O the Magnificent.

Fellow Superior Squad members: Bug Boy, Weasel Woman, Captain Squid, Lure Lass, and Plasmo the Mystic.

Radioactive Man's love interest: The suspicious and gorgeous reporter Gloria Grand.

Secret headquarters: The Containment Dome, just below the summit of Mt. Zenith.

Substitute Earth version: Radioactive Boy and his Radioactive Dog, Glowy.

Played on TV by: Dirk Richter as Radioactive Man, Buddy Hodges as Fallout Boy

Played in ill-fated movie by: Rainier Wolfcastle as Radioactive Man, Milhouse Van Houten as Fallout Boy.

RADIOACTIVE MAN RULES! HE NEVER PUNCHES A BAD GUY WITHOUT SAYING SOMETHING SUPER COOL.

The explosion of an X-ray machine at a Halloween candy inspection releases a bolt of radiation, transforming Bart and Lisa into Stretch Dude and Clobber Girl. With his ability to elongate any part of his body he wishes and her incredible super strength, Bart and Lisa become crime-fighting super heroes with their own TV show.

Quotes: (Stretch Dude) "I must only use this power to annoy."
(Clobber Girl) "Hold the funeral, Poindexter!"

Foes: Bank robbers, Saddam Hussein, Nazi dirigibles, and various forces of evil.

Arch-Nemesis: The Collector.

The Collector's Mylar-encased prisoners: Spock, Gilligan, "Lost in Space" robot, Matt Groening, Dr. Who, Yasmine Bleeth, and Lucy Lawless.

The Collector's witty taunts: Retch Dude and Slobber Girl.

Mode of travel: Clobber Girl pogo-sticks on Stretch Dude.

Stretch Dude's fringe benefits: Rakes leaves with own hand as rake, easily retrieves wristwatch from toilet pipes, limitlessly extends Wet Willie range.

Surprising fact: Lucy Lawless, TV's Xena, can actually fly.

Ralph's shocking candy X-ray reveals: Razor blade, syringe, and white chocolat

AT LAST, WHAT I'VE ALWAYS WANTED, MY OWN TV SHOW!

To attain his dream of retirement at age 12, Bart creates Angry Dad, a comic character based on Homer's towering rages. The least provocation goads Angry Dad into a virulent and destructive fury that the entire worldwide web can enjoy at BetterThanTV.com. Crudely and explosively drawn, Angry Dad is a timely reminder that expressing your rage freely is not just fun, it's also healthy.

Quote: "I hate them so much!"

Incitements to anger: Stopped-up ketchup bottles, losing the remote, newspapers that publish opinions—not news, "The Boring World of Niels Bohr," carpet stores that charge extra for under-padding.

Anger antidote: Bubble bath, candles, soft music, and Churchill Downers Horse Tranquilizers.

Critical acclaim for "Angry Dad": "A timeless comic character!"—Jimbo Jones; "Angry Dad rocks!"—Kearney; "Rack-worthy!"—Comic Book Guy

Production: A Bartoon Presentation in association with Ay Carumba Entertainment.

Internet ratings: #1 non-porn site (10 trillionth overall).

Other BetterThanTV.com features: "Bin Laden in a Blender," "Lou Rawls, Secret Agent."

WHEN CREATING A MASTERPIECE, STINK LINES AROUND THE BUTT PROVIDE JUST THE RIGHT FINISHING TOUCH.

LITTLE KNOWN FACT:

Embarrassed by his roots, Bart plans to change his name to Steve Bennett when he is older.

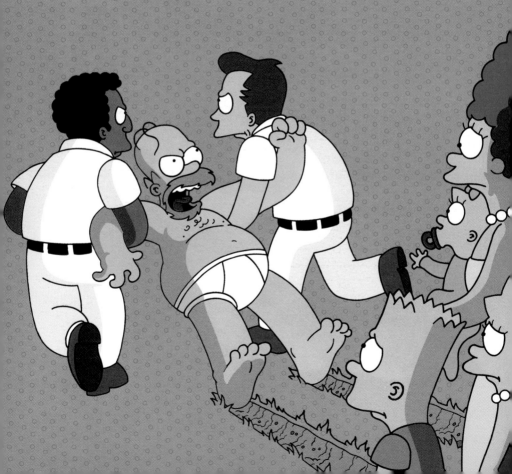

MORE PULLABLE PRANKS

TEST A FRIEND'S "BALANCE" BY PLACING TWO FULL PAPER CUPS OF LIQUID ON THE BACK OF EACH OF HIS HANDS. SAY "YOU'VE PASSED THE TEST!" THEN LEAVE YOUR FRIEND TO FIGURE OUT HOW TO GET THE CUPS OFF OF HIS HANDS WITHOUT SPILLING THE WATER. (HINT: TRY TO DO THIS WHEN NOBODY ELSE IS AROUND TO HELP HIM.) AND NO FAIR TICKLING!

THE OL' SWITCHEROO

Hide a school textbook inside a comic book. It will confuse your teacher when she comes to investigate and sees you doing your homework. (Danger! Be prepared to have the comic book confiscated anyway!)

Looking to waste a little time? Annoy a few adults? Cause a friend to blow milk out his nose? Nothing on earth beats...

...FUN WITH FACIAL MUSCLES!

Peptic Ulcer Man

The Anteater

Raspberrio

The Hully Gully

The Moron

Gaggerella

The Howler Monkey

Belchasaurus

Mr. Wonderful

The Flanders

El Monstro

The Shriveler

The Mutilator

Phantom of the Opera

The Space Mutant

The Wombat

The Wild and Crazy Guy

STOP THAT NOW!

Mom

BART'S RECIPES FOR

#32 - CONVENIENT CLASSIC

1. Call a local convenience store.
2. Ask the clueless clock-puncher on the other end of the phone, "Do you have Prince Albert in a can?"
3. When he/she answers, "Yes, we do." say, "You'd better let him out before he suffocates!"
4. Cackle like a jackal and hang up.

Caution! You may want to case the store in advance to make sure they do sell Prince Albert tobacco. Otherwise, be prepared with a backup question, such as:

Q: "Do you carry Dolley Madison?"
A: "What's the matter? Are her legs broken?"

TELEPHONE FUN

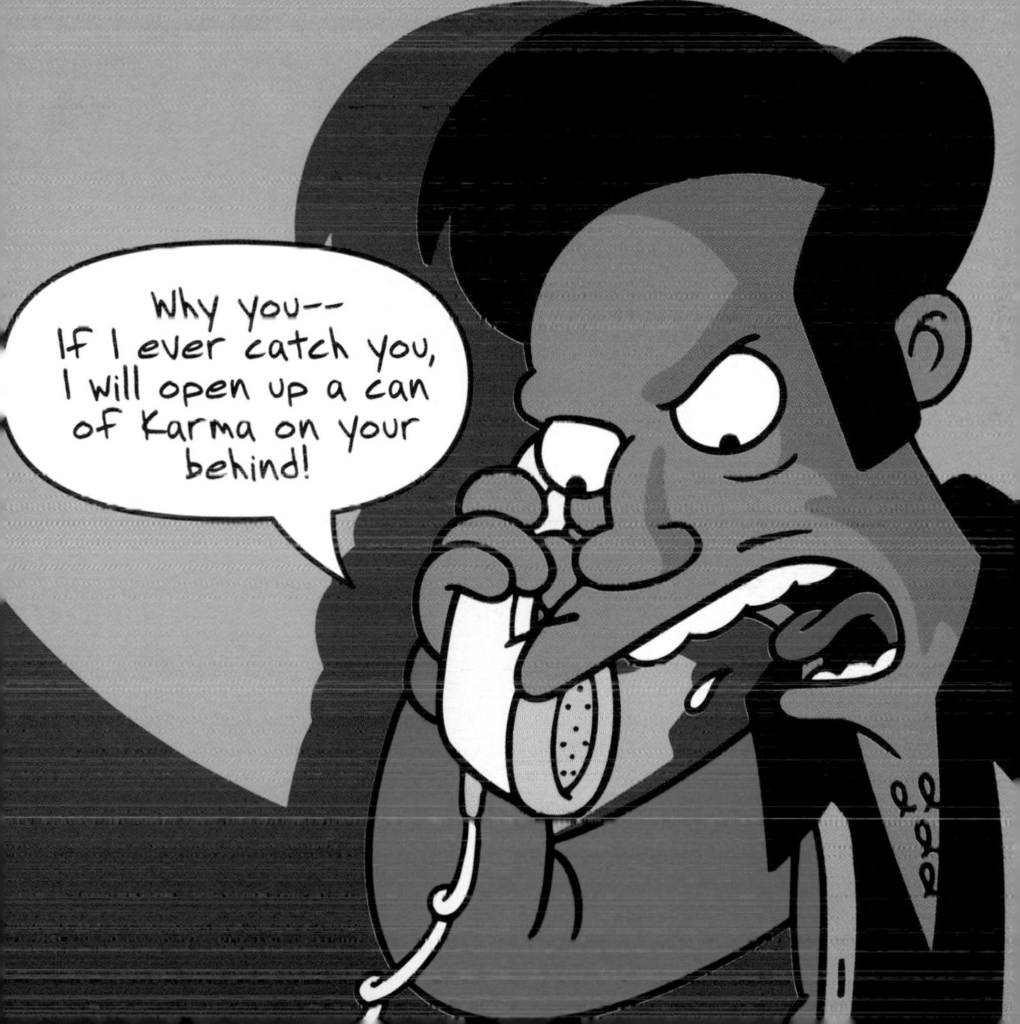
Why you--
If I ever catch you, I will open up a can of Karma on your behind!

A TYPICAL DAY IN THE LIFE

7:00 a.m. – Bart hits snooze button twice on his Krusty Klock® alarm clock. When it goes off again saying, "Hey, hey! What am I, your mother?" he gets up.

7:15 a.m. – Bart/Lisa reach bathroom at same time. Instead of engaging in same old fight, he plays gentleman/gestures for her to go first/gives her good-morning noogie from behind.

7:30 a.m. – Time to get dressed. Bart decides to wear blue T-shirt today, but realizes he does not own one.

7:45 a.m. – From bathroom window, Bart moons Flanders family as their car pulls out of driveway. Distracted Ned runs over mailbox...again.

8:00 a.m. – Breakfast is served! For morning energy, Bart eats big, heaping bowl of Krusty Brand® Korn Syrup Klusters–"The cereal that dilates your eyes."

8:30 a.m. – School bus picks up Bart/Lisa. During ride, Bart sneaks box of colored chalk into Ralph Wiggum's lunch pail, hoping he will eat it.

8:45 a.m. – As school bus passes Chief Wiggum in patrol car, Bart moons him. Wiggum vows to catch perpetrator, but fails to write down license number of suspect's vehicle in time.

9:00 a.m. – First school bell rings. Previous night's Science homework assignment was "Do people do stupid things while under duress?" Bart attempts to answer question by "scientifically" shooting Ping-Pong balls at Milhouse's head with air bazooka.

9:15 a.m. – Bart asks Mrs. Krabappel for permission to go to bathroom. Staring contest ensues. Bart wins/gets hall pass. Mrs. K makes mental note: "Try harder to break Bart's spirit."

9:30 a.m. – Passes open door of Principal Skinner's office. Witnesses Skinner's mother handcuffing him to his desk as punishment for dodging after-school girdle-shopping date on previous day.

9:45 a.m. – Skinner gives Bart his ATM card/PIN number; instructs him to buy hacksaw at hardware store–thus proving people do stupid things while under duress.

10:00 a.m. – Takes maximum amount possible out of Skinner's bank account—$20.

10:15 a.m. – At Kwik-E-Mart, buys Triple Fudgie, pack of Uh-Ohs, Jumbo Blam!-Berry Squishee; gets dollar in quarters/plays Time Waster IV video game.

10:30 a.m. – Leaves Kwik-E-Mart, passing Homer on way out; they exchange polite pleasantries.

10:45 a.m. – Sneaks inside his house while Marge vacuums, grabs Homer's toolbox from garage. Also dusts Homer's clean underwear with chili powder/puts them back in drawer.

11:00 a.m. – Returns to school for last few minutes of recess. Uses wrench from toolbox to loosen bolts on swings. Much sand-eating follows.

11:15 a.m. – Bart intends to skip assembly to rescue Skinner, but Professor Frink brings in big plant that smells like "dead body." Bart shuts off assembly hall lights, shoves plant into air conditioning duct.

11:30 a.m. – Most everyone waits outside while Groundskeeper Willie hunts through air ducts to find smelly plant. Bart stays inside/Xeroxes 200 copies of his butt.

11:45 a.m. – After classes return to normal, Bart spends time driving Lisa crazy making faces at her from outside classroom door. Miss Hoover threatens to put him in hamster cage if he doesn't move along.

12:00 p.m. – Lunchtime! Today's special: Barbecue Surprise. With leftover smell of corpse plant wafting through cafeteria, none of the students are in mood for any sort of surprise.

12:15 p.m. – Ralph Wiggum puts on big show of his multi-colored teeth/says his throw-up was same colors.

12:30 p.m. – Kickball game–"Shirts vs. Skins." Skins team-captain Bart repeatedly stands directly behind teammate Uter, reaches around, makes Uter's belly/bosoms jiggle; hypnotized Shirts lose game.

1:00 p.m. – Bart surrounded by bullies in hallway. Action moves to Boys' Lavatory, where they steal Homer's toolbox. Indian burns/wedgies/swirlies follow.

1:15 p.m. – Picks lock to Groundskeeper Willie's tool shed to get another hacksaw. Finds hidden tunnel inside/follows it to Willie's secret underground lair. Wonders if Willie is evil super-villain/alien from outer space; disappointed when he finds only stamp collection/old vinyl records.

1:30 p.m. – Notices several tunnels lead out of Willie's lair/takes different one back. Comes out in Girls' Gym in middle of volleyball class/moons girls/runs out.

1:45 p.m. – Back in class, it is time for Math. Bart puts face in hands/moans. He forgot to bring Math homework to school. Also, did not do Math homework.

2:00 p.m. – Krabappel calls Bart to front of class to solve division problem. Thinking fast, Bart uses Willie's hacksaw to divide Krabappel's chalkboard pointer into thirds. Krabappel illustrates theory of subtraction by sending Bart to Principal's office.

2:15 p.m. – Superintendent Chalmers is in Skinner's office when Bart arrives. Chalmers remarks how unusual it is that Skinner contracted "lock-knees"/cannot stand up. Skinner promises to catch rowdy students who removed bumpers from Chalmer's car—one named "Homer" left toolbox behind.

2:30 p.m. – Bart saws through handcuffs, sets Skinner free. With mere moments to spare, Skinner hides in closet when his mother arrives. Bart rats Skinner out.

2:45 p.m. – Bart writes "IN THE OLD DAYS, SNITCHES GOT FRAGGED" on chalkboard one hundred times.

3:00 p.m. – School's out! Bart skateboards home through park where Springfield Daughters of the American Revolution are holding picnic; he moons them.

3:15 p.m. – Rendezvous with Milhouse in treehouse, peruse *Medical Blunders* magazine found in trash until they get too grossed-out.

3:30 p.m. – Bart/Milhouse take Santa's Little Helper for walk. Bart convinces Grampa/ other old people at Springfield Retirement Castle that Santa's Little Helper is bomb-sniffing dog; he declares their medicine ball is rigged with explosives. Abe panics/calls bomb squad.

3:45 p.m. – Bomb squad (Chief Wiggum in a hockey mask) arrives as Bart/Milhouse sneak away/run back to Bart's house. Bart tricks Milhouse into thinking unmarked police cars circling block. Makes Milhouse promise to hide with dog in doghouse until Bart returns later with "all clear" signal.

4:00 p.m. – Watches afternoon children's TV/puts brain on "standby" for two hours.

6:00 p.m. – Jarred back to reality when Kent Brockman comes on. Slow news day: top story features video of Homer guiltily putting bumpers back on Chalmers' car, as police stand around smacking open palms with batons.

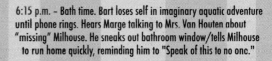

6:15 p.m. – Bath time. Bart loses self in imaginary aquatic adventure until phone rings. Hears Marge talking to Mrs. Van Houten about "missing" Milhouse. He sneaks out bathroom window/tells Milhouse to run home quickly, reminding him to "Speak of this to no one."

6:30 p.m. – Since he only wears a towel, Bart stands on street mooning passing cars.

6:45 p.m. – Dinner is served. This evening's fare: Marge's Meatloaf Surprise. Homer is not in mood for any more "surprises" today.

7:00 p.m. – Time for English homework: essay on plight of "post-Industrial Age" Man. Bart optimistically opens notebook to blank page.

7:30 p.m. – Stares at the blank page.

7:45 p.m. – Continues to stare at blank page.

8:00 p.m. – Glances out window. Crazy Old Man from Grampa's retirement home moons him. Extremely disturbed, Bart shudders/wonders why someone would do that.

9:15 p.m. – Declares homework assignment "stupid"/decides to turn in early. Although tired from full day, sleep is elusive. Feels as if he's forgotten something.

9:18 p.m. – Realizes he still has Skinner's ATM card. Calls/orders *Medical Blunders* magazine subscription for Skinner. Mission accomplished, Bart drifts off to sleep, knowing he has had "a very productive day."

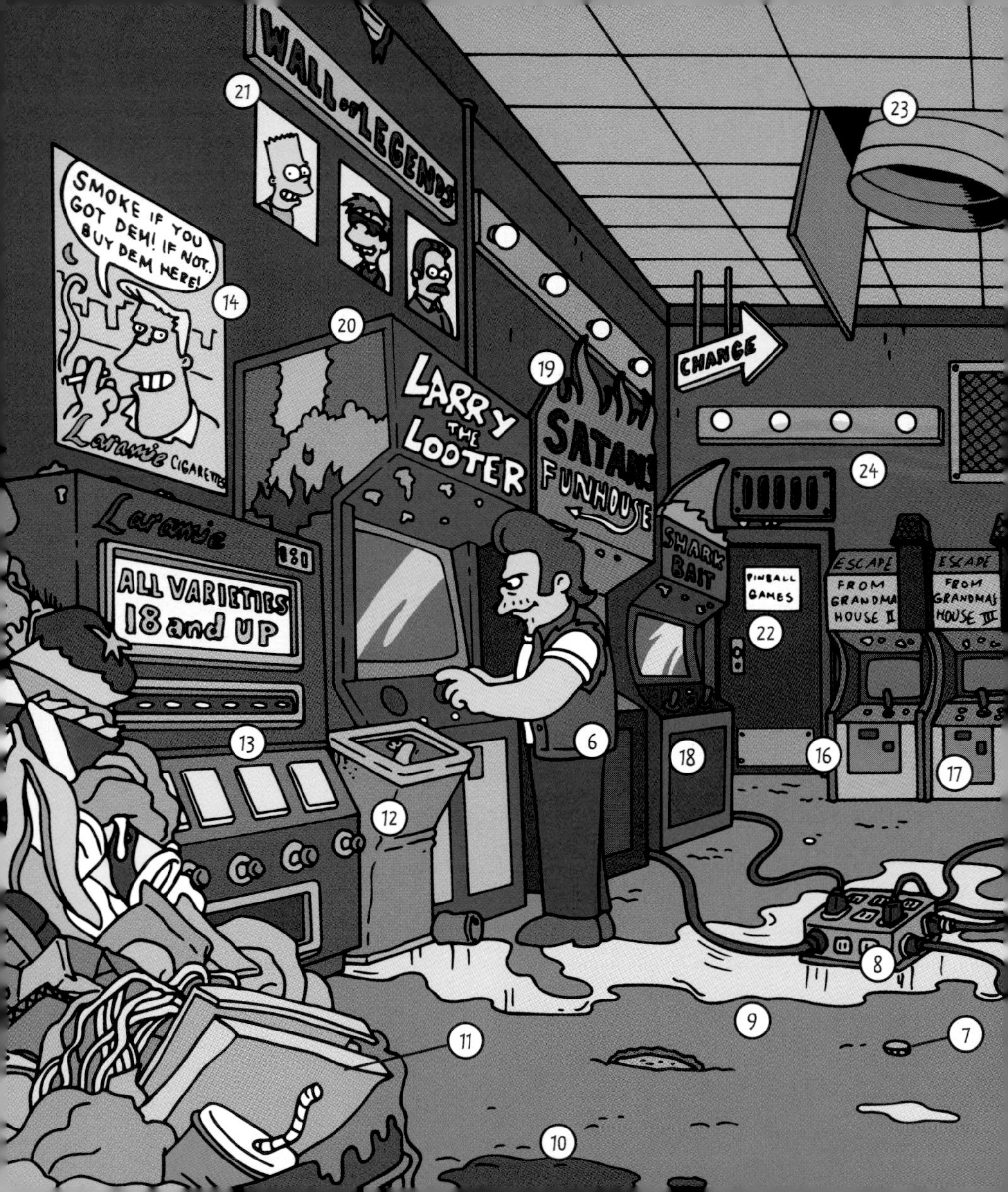

WALL OF LEGENDS
SMOKE IF YOU GOT DEM! IF NOT.. BUY DEM HERE!
Laramie CIGARETTES
Laramie
ALL VARIETIES 18 and UP
LARRY THE LOOTER
SATAN'S FUNHOUSE
SHARK BAIT
CHANGE
PINBALL GAMES
ESCAPE FROM GRANDMA'S HOUSE II
ESCAPE FROM GRANDMA'S HOUSE III
21
23
14
20
19
24
22
13
6
18
16
17
12
8
9
11
7
10

BART ZONES
NOISELAND ARCADE

1. Change booth.
2. God.
3. Restroom. (Use only if desperate!)
4. My Dinner With André video game.
5. Burnouts.
6. Future of the burnouts.
7. A QUARTER! LOOK, A QUARTER!
8. Vital Electrical Safety Device (surge protector).
9. Original carpeting from the '60s (listed on the historic registers of both the National Interior Design Board and the Centers for Disease Control).
10. Buzz Cola stain. (We hope.)
11. Rarely emptied trash can.
12. Drinking fountain.
13. Laramie Cigarettes vending machine.
14. Endorsement from celebrity role model.
15. Thick layer of dust.
16. Escape From Grandma's House II video game.
17. Escape from Grandma's House III: The Great Thanksgiving Disaster
18. Shark Bait video game.
19. Satan's Funhouse video game. ("You can exchange your soul for quarters at the desk!")
20. The Franchise.
21. Wall of Legends.
22. Nerd holding area.
23. Air conditioning vent (pumps oxygen to keep kids alert).
24. Indescribable all-pervasive funk.

NELSON MUNTZ 4TH GRADE BULLY

A riddle wrapped in an enigma wrapped in a vest, Nelson Muntz is both a figurehead of menace in the community and a role model for young misguided rebels. If you're not careful he'll break your nose, your glasses, and your heart. A born bully with a talent for thievin', Nelson has been held back in 4th grade so often that he has to shave during detention.

Quote: "Haw Haw! I'm wicked bad!"

Purpose in life: To teach all sissy wimps a lesson.

Pet peeve: No one appreciates his sensitive side.

Secret shame: Not as smart as he looks.

Special offer: A recess and lunch protection package that's very affordable.

Culinary specialty: Muntz Family Chili. ("It Takes Weeks to Make Muntz.")

Schoolyard specialties: Hot Foots, Wedgies, Slime Wedgies, Pink Bellies, Hertz Donuts, and the dreaded Rear Admiral.

Hobbies: Pantsing people, wasting squirrels with BB guns, decorating neighbors' homes with coleslaw.

Marks of distinction: Diplomatic immunity in Springfield Elementary's Model United Nations, banned for life from The Android's Dungeon.

WHILE MORALLY WRONG, BULLYING IS AN ANCIENT ART. IT PREDATES AGRICULTURE.

DOLPH, KEARNEY & JIMBO PETTY THUGS, BULLIES, AND LOWLIFES

The product of broken homes, much of which they broke themselves, Jimbo, Dolph and Kearney love nothing better than beating up science geeks and taking their lunch money—though they wouldn't try it alone. Noted for their slovenly attire and greasy good looks, they roam the neighborhood in a pack, sneaking into movies, shoplifting at the local Kwik-E-Mart, and stealing bumper cars from Duff Gardens.

Quote: (Jimbo) "I heard that guy's ass has its own congressman."
(Dolph) "You asked for it, man! You're broadcasting geek rays all over the entire valley."
(Kearney) "First one to blink is a dead man."

Pecking order: Jimbo, Kearney, Dolph.

Pet peeves: Paying for stuff, stop signs.

Favorite author: Bazooka Joe.

Typical meal: Beef jerky, a Jumbo Squishee, and a squirt of Binaca.

Hobbies: Five finger discounts, flushing cherry bombs, cheesing people off, and smearing door handles with peanut butter.

Disclaimer: They don't bully girls because they bite and kick and scratch. And they might fall in love.

Summer employment: Kounselors at Kamp Krusty.

Did you know?: Jimbo's real first name is "Corky," Kearney has been held back in school so often he has a young son, and Dolph likes talking to clouds.

Their motto: If you can't say anything nice about anybody, you're okay by me.

YOU'VE GOT TO HAND IT TO THEM. THEY ADVANCED THE ART OF THE WEDGIE INTO THE 21ST CENTURY.

MILHOUSE VAN HOUTEN BART'S BEST FRIEND AND SPITBROTHER

A self-confessed second banana, Milhouse is Bart's big-nosed, bespectacled best friend and loyal sidekick. While Milhouse fancies himself as hip, smart, and soulful, he gets cranky when he misses his juice and cries when the cafeteria runs out of chocolate milk. A willing, yet unwitting victim of Bart's shenanigans, Milhouse is also victimized by a burning unrequited love for Lisa who thinks of him as "more like a big sister."

Quote: "My mom says I'm cool."

Secret identity: Bartman's sidekick, Houseboy.

Secret ambition: To have sideburns even bushier than Carl Yastrzemski's.

Secret shame: Actually likes brussels sprouts.

Prized possessions: Zipper-encrusted leather jacket acquired by trading in bubble gum wrappers, "My Little Pony" plush doll, and Bart's soul.

Allergies: Knuckle sandwiches, lactose intolerance.

Turn-ons: 100% All-Syrup Super Squishees, Gummi in all its wondrous forms, and making grease angels on the kitchen floor.

"Weekend Dad": Kirk Van Houten.

"Weekday Dad": Pyro from "American Gladiators."

Hard-won insight: Discovered while playing "Fallout Boy" that stardom is hollow and meaningless.

I DON'T CARE IF YOUR MOM SAYS I'M A BAD INFLUENCE, MILHOUSE. HOW MANY TIMES HAVE I TOLD YOU? NEVER LISTEN TO YOUR MOTHER!

LAURA POWERS BART'S NEXT DOOR NEIGHBOR & FIRST LOVE

Laura Powers is a tough-talkin', good-lookin' Army brat who can turn a young rebel's heart to mush in the time it takes to give you a Hertz Donut. She speaks politely to adults when necessary, teaches cats to waltz, and makes even belches seem alluring. After just one look and a couple of Wet Willies, Bart makes the ultimate sacrifice for her—he takes a bath.

Quote: "If you were old enough to grow a bad teenage mustache, I'd go out with you in a second."

Claim to fame: Can spit farther than any boy.

Secret shame: Enjoys wearing dresses.

Upbringing: Painfully strict.

Favorite Restaurant: Two Guys from Kabul.

Odd jobs: Babysitting, telling fortunes, and dance instructing.

Likes: Good-looking rebels who play by their own rules, poking dead bodies with a stick, and messing with your mind.

Dislikes: Authority, disco, and—in the "Escape from Death Row" video game—when you hit the change of venue button and end up in Texas.

SOMETIMES A GUY JUST LIKES HIS SKIN TO LOOK ITS YELLOWEST.

ITCHY & SCRATCHY HILARIOUSLY VIOLENT CARTOON MOUSE & CAT

Itchy is a homicidal sadistic cartoon mouse, who cheerfully impales, lacerates, crushes, and explodes his perpetually unwitting victim, Scratchy the Cat. Educational as well as entertaining, Itchy & Scratchy cartoons prove there are more than one hundred ways to skin a cat—all of them chock-full of merriment and screaming. And though Scratchy may die myriad bloody and shriek-tacular deaths, he lives to die another day.

Quote: (Itchy) "Immolation is the highest form of flattery."
(Scratchy) "A rolling stone slaughters no mouse."

Shakespeare Itchy & Scratchy style: "The Maiming of the Shrew," "A Midsummer Night's Scream," "Romeo and Thumb-Screwliet."

Official spokespersons for: Buzz Cola. ("Drink Buzz or We'll Kill You.")

Amusement park: Itchy & Scratchy Land—The Violentest Place on Earth!

Full length movies: "Scratchtasia," "Pinitchyo," and "Itchy & Scratchy: The Movie."

Members of the Itchy & Scratchy family: Brown-Nose Bear, Disgruntled goat, Flatulent Fox, Rich Uncle Skeleton, Dinner Dog, Uncle Ant, and Ku Klux Clam.

Zen koan: If you exploded a cat in the forest and there was no one there to hear it, would it make a shriek?

Scratchy first introduced: "That Happy Cat" (1928).

First Itchy & Scratchy cartoon: "Steamboat Itchy" (1929).

Controversy: Chester J. Lampwick claims origin of Itchy in his film "Itchy, The Lucky Mouse in Manhattan Madness" (1919).

ITCHY & SCRATCHY STUDIOS ARE VERY CONCERNED ABOUT VIOLENCE. THEY'RE ALWAYS CAREFUL TO SHOW THE CONSEQUENCES OF DEADLY MAYHEM SO THAT THEY MAY EDUCATE AS WELL AS HORRIFY.

William "Fat Tony" Williams, AKA Anthony D'Amico, AKA Marion D'Amico heads up a loose organization of unorthodox businessmen. He is a force to be reckoned with due to his ability to offer public services not normally found in the yellow pages, including: smuggling, bookmaking, protection services, numbers running, loan sharking, document forging, and racketeering. Fat Tony's Rat Pack-lifestyle exerts an irresistible pull on Bart, who signs on, temporarily, as Fat Tony's bartender.

Quote: "If you do not wish to arouse suspicion, I strongly urge you to act American."

Hangout: The Legitimate Businessman's Social Club.

Henchmen: Legs, Louie and Joey.

Godfather: Don Vittorio.

Hobbies: Handicapping horse races, poker playing, and collecting debts.

Most frequent poker hand: Five Aces.

Special skills: Taking the 5th, lying to grand juries, delegating responsibility for murder, and eluding elementary school hall monitors.

Businesses: Valdazzo Brother's Olive Oil, Lowball Construction, Squeaky Farms Dairy Products.

Specialty equipment: An ice pick with a laser sight.

Favorite beverage: The Manhattan, the King of Cocktails.

Portraiture: Graces walls of numerous post offices, municipal buildings, and counterfeit currency.

DO ME A FAVOR, FAT TONY, DON'T DO ME ANY MORE FAVORS.

 If you ask me, everybody wants to be a free-spirited individual. But, on the other hand, nobody wants to be alienated from their peer group. That's why God made tattoos! Nothing says "I'm a wild non-conformist who's terrified of not fitting in!" quite like a tattoo! This one on my arm is phony, but I can't wait 'til I'm old enough to get inked for real! In fact, I've already got my designs ready and waiting. Check 'em out, man!

BART'S TATTOO REVUE

MOTHER

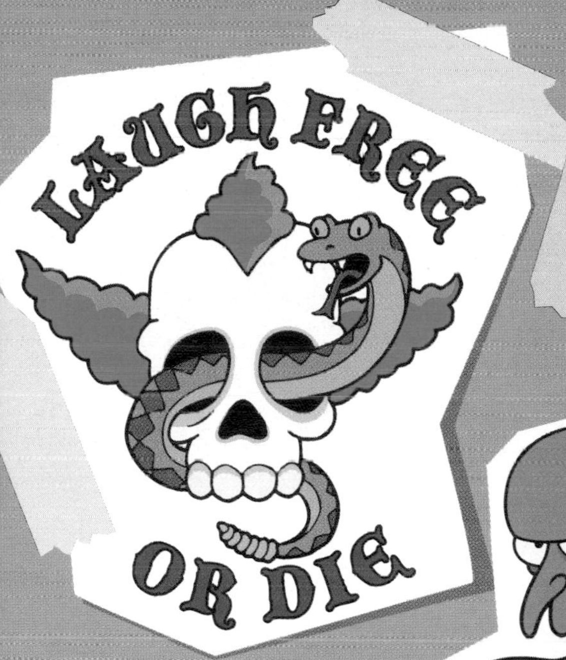
LAUGH FREE
OR DIE

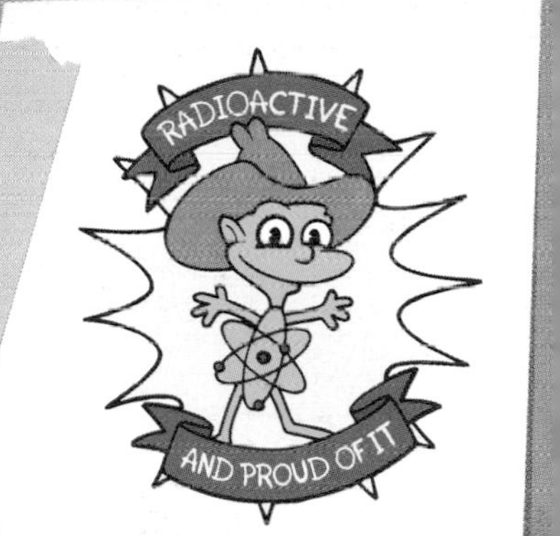
RADIOACTIVE
AND PROUD OF IT

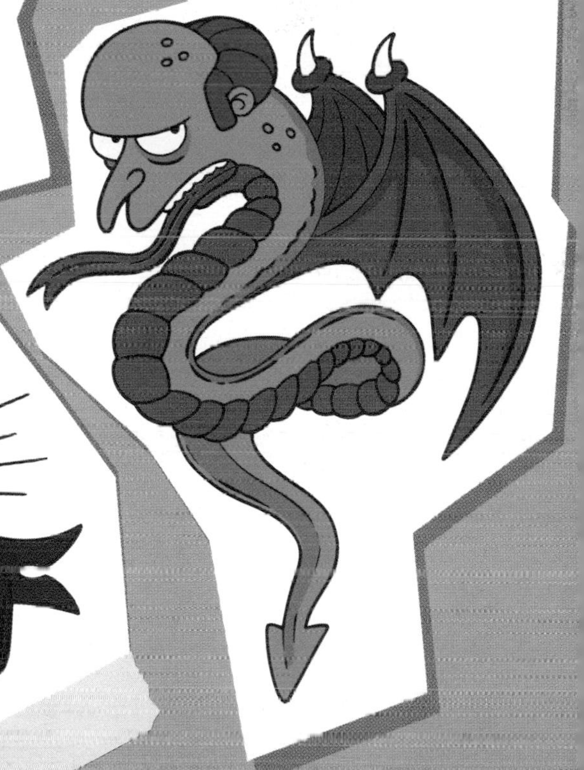

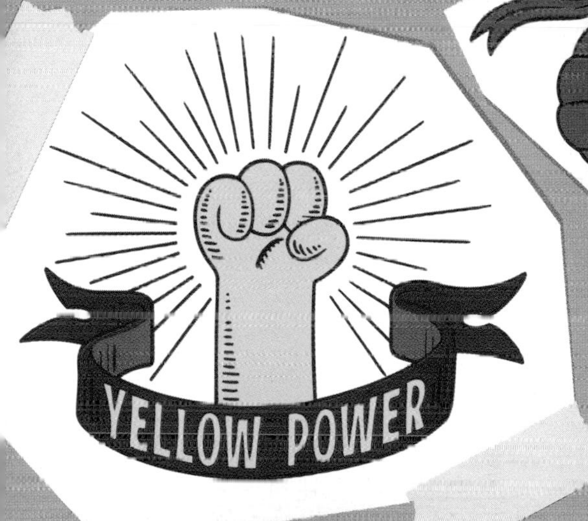
YELLOW POWER

Don't Mess With El Barto

In Loving Memory

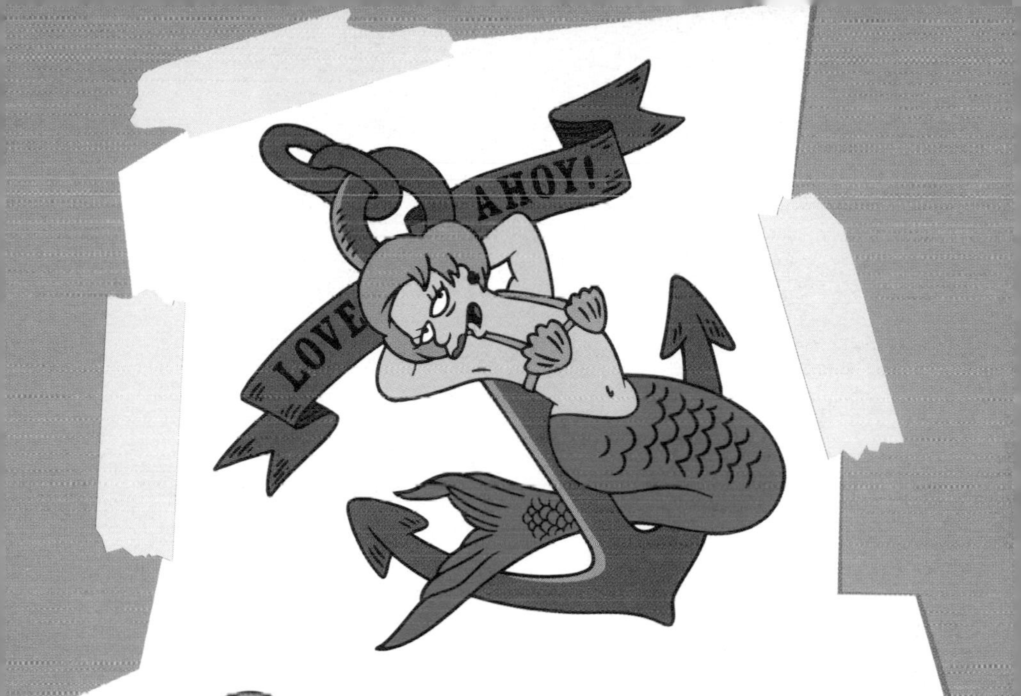
LOVE AHOY!

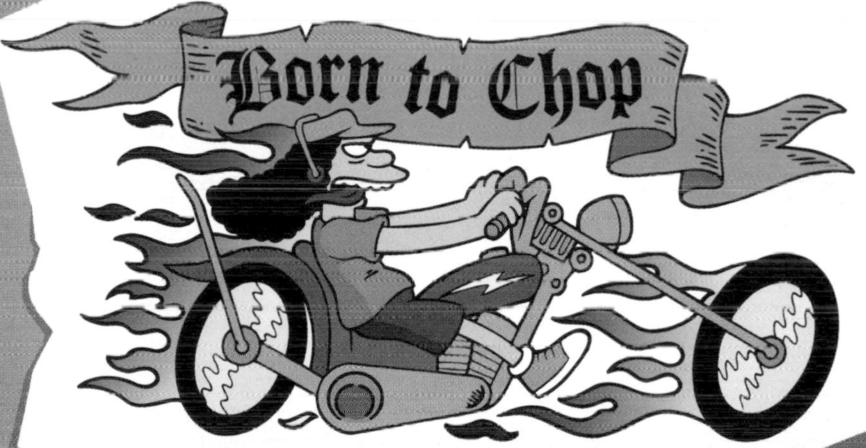
Born to Chop

BART'S RECIPES FOR

#49 - POTTY TALK

1. Call the schmoe of your choice.
2. Ask the victim "Is there a John there?"
3. When they answer "I'm sorry, there's no John here" say, "Well how do you go to the bathroom?"
4. Giggle like The Joker and hang up.

Caution! Unless you enjoy working without a net, make sure there isn't actually a person named John living or working with your target!

TELEPHONE FUN

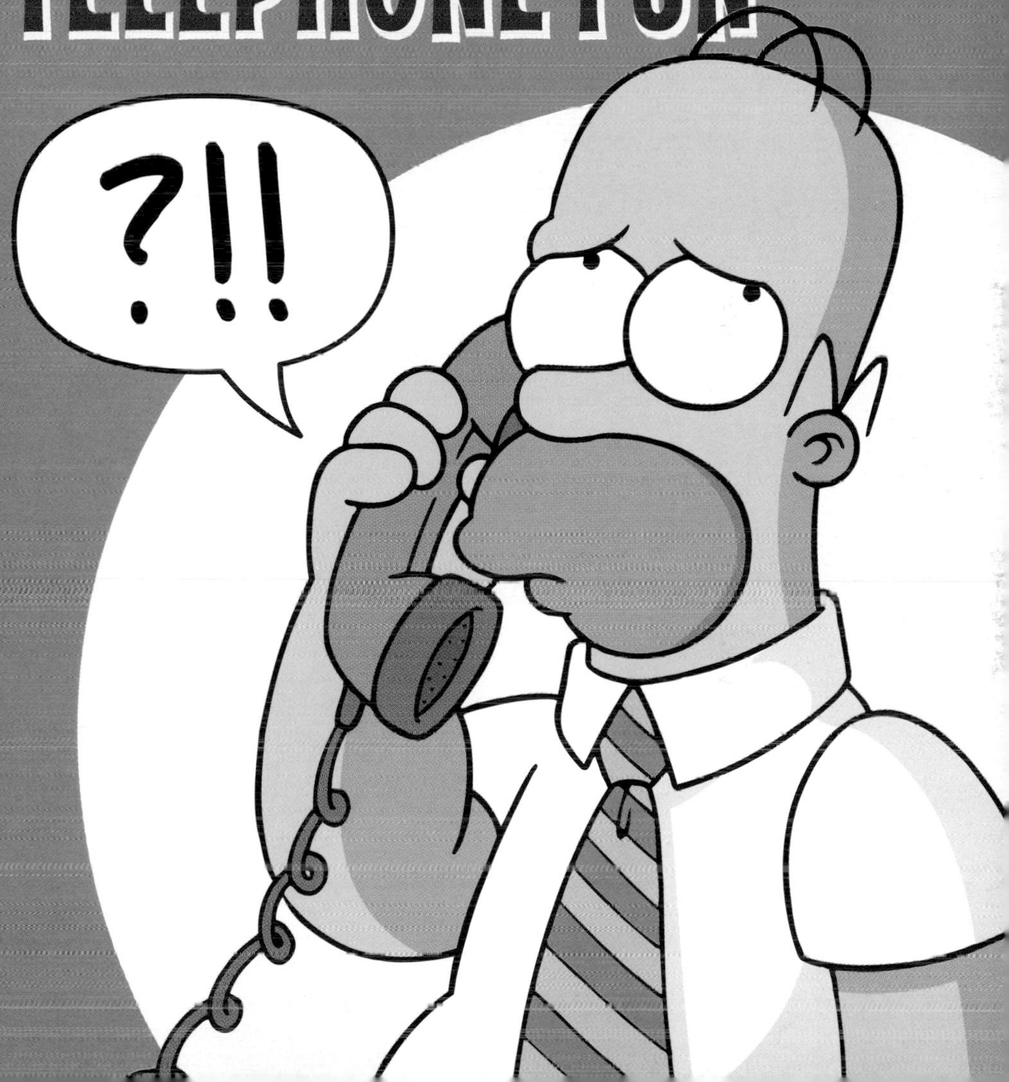
?!!

LITTLE KNOWN FACT:

Between the two of them, Bart and Milhouse have read the first 814 issues of Radioactive Man.

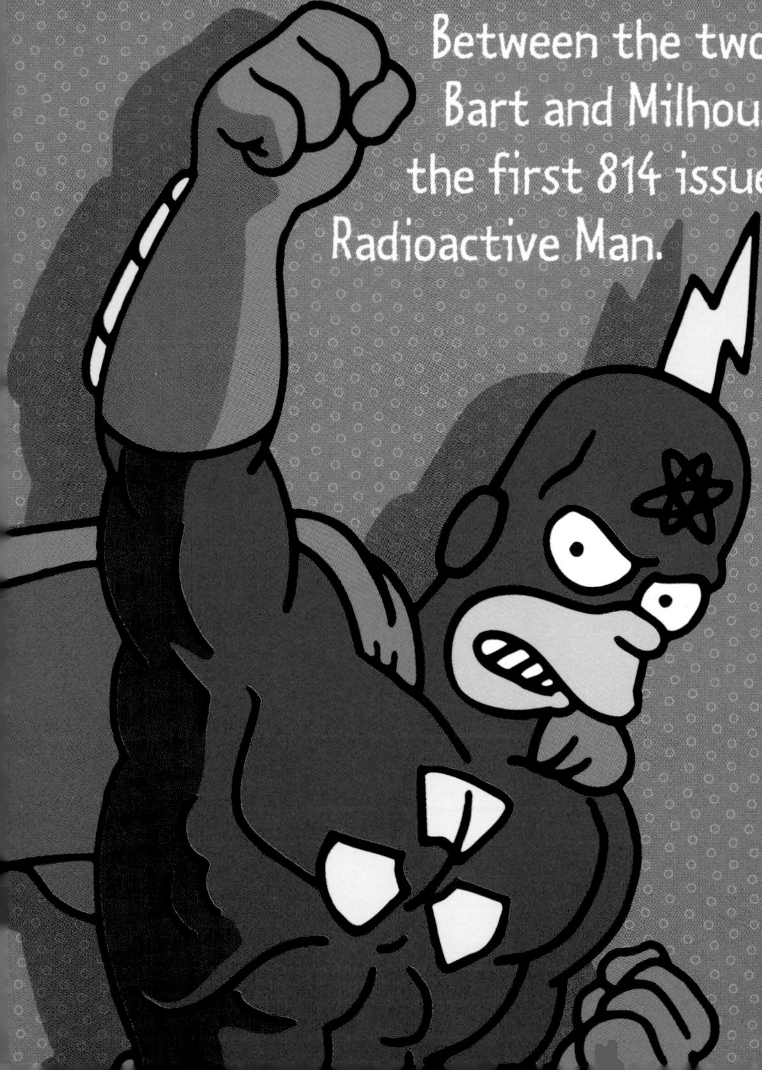

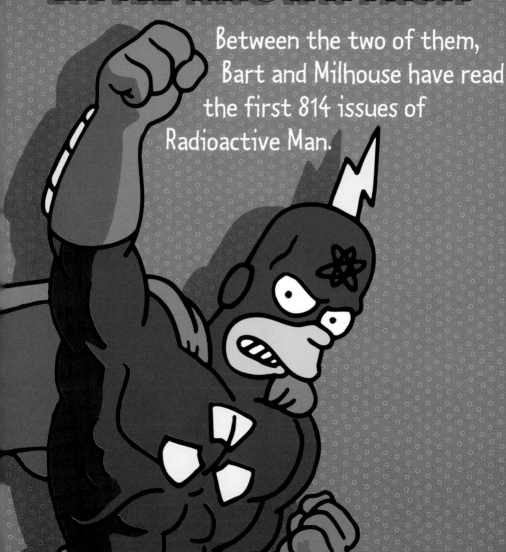

STILL MORE PULLABLE PRANKS

The Classic Corner – SHORTSHEETING THE BED

Here's one trick that's been part of our cultural heritage for generations, practiced in houses and summer camps the world over. Follow the easy steps below.

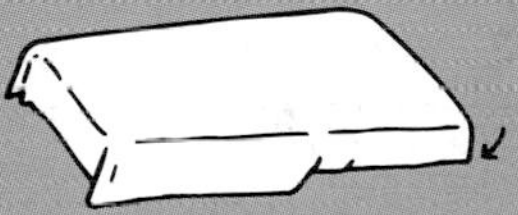

FIG. 1 – Take the top sheet off the bed and lay it loosely over the fitted bottom sheet. Tuck the top half under the mattress so it looks like a fitted bottom sheet.

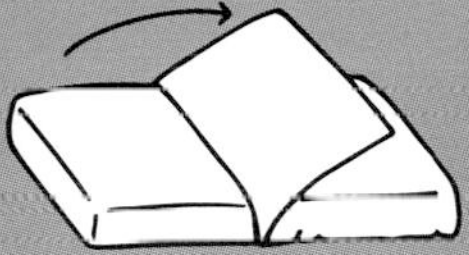

FIG. 2 – Fold the bottom half up to look like a normal top sheet, creating a pocket for a person to fit in.

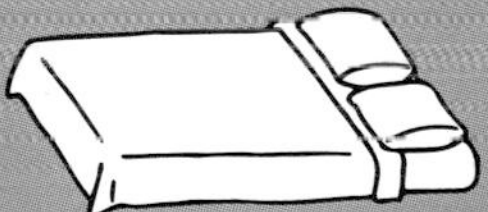

FIG. 3 – To camouflage your handiwork, make up the rest of the bed as usual.

FIG. 4 – When the unsuspecting slumberer tries to go to bed, they'll only be able to fit in halfway!

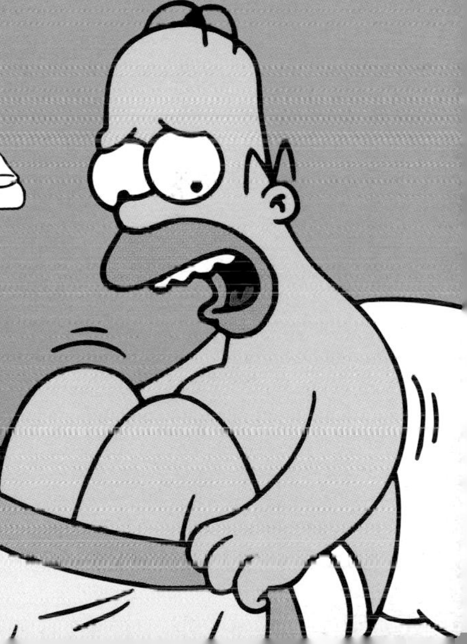
HEY! WHAT TH--?!

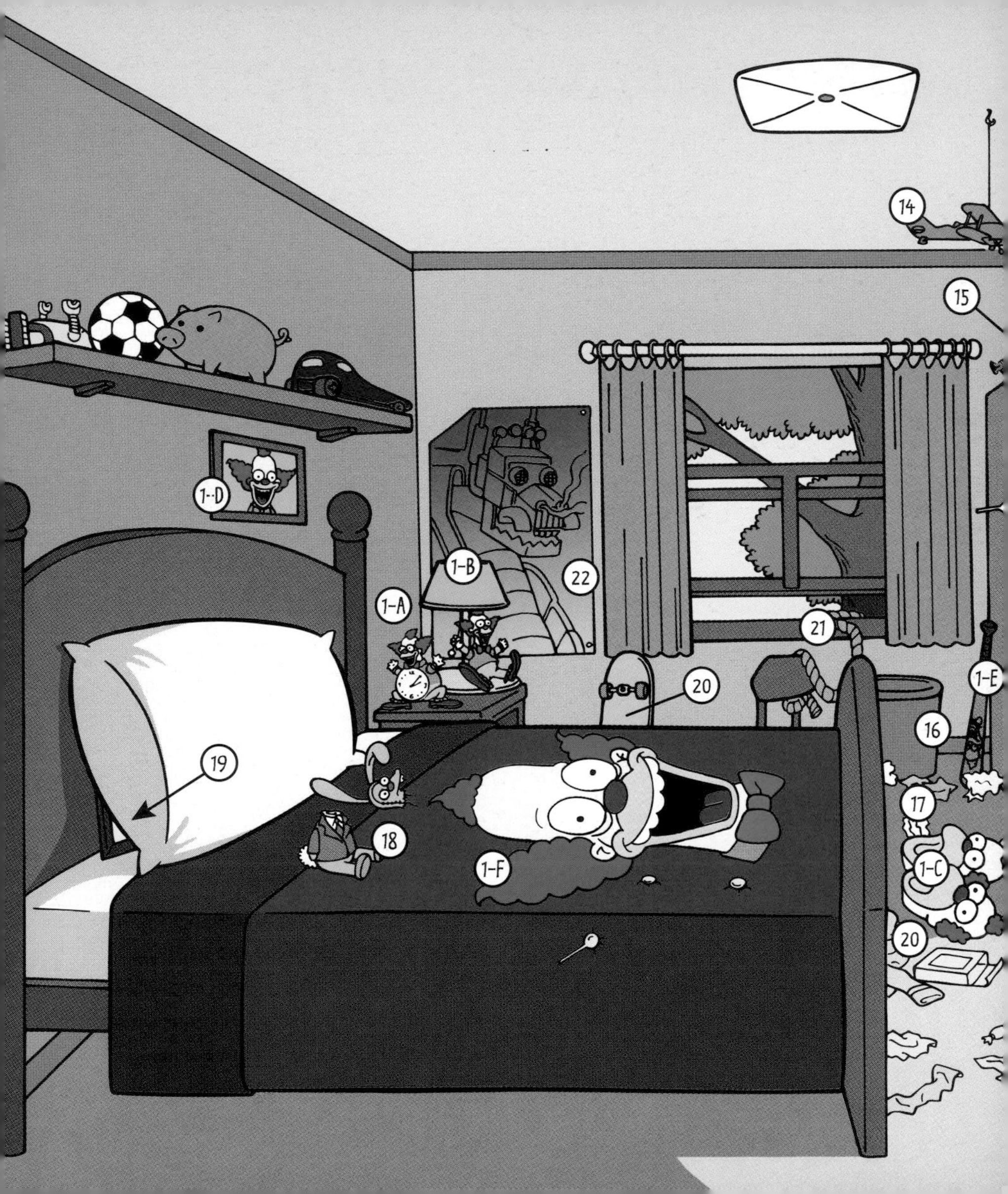
14
15
1-D
1-B
22
1-A
21
20
1-E
16
19
17
18
1-C
1-F
20

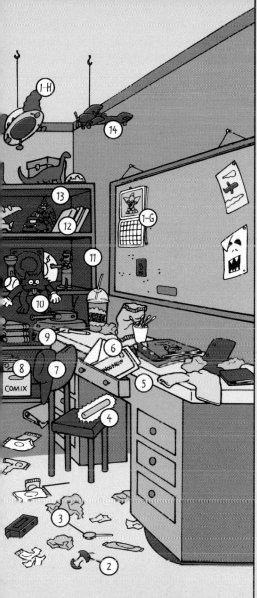

BART ZONES
BART'S BEDROOM

1. All Things KRUSTY. **A)** Krusty Alarm Klock, **B)** Krusty Bedside Lamp, **C)** Krusty Slippers, **D)** Krusty Photo, **E)** Krusty Baseball Bat, **F)** Krusty Bedsheets, **G)** Krusty Wall Kalendar, **H)** Krusty Brand Space Probe.
2. Emergency Food Supply.
3. Candy.
4. Plutonium rod (one of the benefits of having a father in the business).
5. Center of Learning and Inquiry.
6. Love letters from Mrs. Krabappel (addressed to Woodrow).
7. Lucky red cap.
8. Investments.
9. Report Card Forgery Device.
10. Scratchy doll (squirts blood when squeezed).
11. Bookshelves ("Technically speaking").
12. Strictly for show.
13. Radioactive Man doll ("With real gamma rays!!!").
14. World War I biplanes.
15. Arsenal.
16. Trash can.
17. Trash.
18. Mr. Honeybunny.
19. Photo of Jessica Lovejoy.
20. Getaway vehicle.
21. Escape plan.
22. Truckasaurus poster.

KRUSTY THE CLOWN ENTREPRENEUR & FUNNYMAN, KRUSTY THE CLOWN SHOW

Krusty the Clown, the "Maitre d' of glee," crafted his first act with jokes he swiped from Yiddles Joke Shop. He then worked as a street mime in Tupelo, Mississippi, and today he heads a shamelessly profitable merchandising empire. Though idolized by Springfield's children, Krusty never remembers their names—even Bart who has saved his bacon numerous times. However, there is one person he remembers without fail—his bookie.

Quote: "I'd like to thank God for all my success, even though I never worshipped or believed in him in any way."

Real name: Herschel Krustofski.

Identifying marks: Green hair, little feet, and a superfluous nipple.

TV rivals: Gabbo, Hobo Hank.

Personal assistant: Lois Pennycandy.

Colleagues: Sideshow Bob, Sideshow Mel, Sideshow Raheem, Corporal Punishment, Mister Teeny.

His signature charity: Telethon for Motion Sickness.

Gold album: "Kroon Along with Krusty"

A sampling of genuine Krusty® Brand Products: Krustyburger Laffy Meals, Krusty Brand Pork Squeezin's, Chocolate Frosted Frosty Krusty Flakes, Uncle Krusty's Tile, Tub and Tonsil Kleaner, Lady Krusty Mustache Removal System, Krusty Non-Toxic Kologne ("For the Smell of the Big Top"), and the second edition of Krusty's International Thesaurus.

Related commercial concerns: KrustyLu Studios, Krustyland Amusement Park, Kamp Krusty—"The Krustiest Place on Earth."

HE'S MY IDOL. I'VE BASED MY WHOLE LIFE ON HIS TEACHINGS.

Adopted on Christmas Eve, Santa's Little Helper is an integral part of the Simpson household: fetching the daily paper and ripping it up, giving a warning bark at the wind, and supplying an endless stream of rich skin-moisturizing drool. In fact, Santa's Little Helper feels so at home he eats meals on the dining room table without even being asked.

Turn-on: Shredded hog snouts in jellied goo.

Turn-off: People breath.

Hobbies: Burying small appliances in the backyard, sniffing butts, sleeping in Homer's hammock.

Secret shame: Holds Springfield Downs record for most consecutive last-place finishes.

Claim to fame: Once fathered a litter of 25 puppies.

Past life: France's Louis the XIV, the Sun King.

Special skills: Can walk while balancing on a ball.

Favorite drinks: A refreshing slurp of toilet water, and gazpacho.

SANTA'S LITTLE HELPER IS SO COOL. WHEN YOU LOOK IN HIS EYES YOU CAN SEE YOURSELF.

LISA SIMPSON BART'S 8-YEAR-OLD SISTER

Lisa is intelligent, sensitive, talented, and creative. As a result, she is an outcast, taken for granted by her teachers and family. Lisa takes solace in her science experiments, academic achievements and especially her saxophone solos, which serve to reconnect her to her family. After which they tell her to go play somewhere else.

Quote: "If Bart got hurt or died, despite the extra attention I'd receive, I'd miss him."

First word: Bart!

Diet: Vegetarian.

Current reading: Virginia Woolf, Zelda Fitzgerald, Sylvia Plath, and "Non-Threatening Boys Magazine."

Turn-ons: Waffles, ponies, and women who have resisted domination by the patriarchy.

Turn-offs: Hypocritical self-serving politicians, environmental degradation, and the music of John Philip Sousa.

Her unholy obsession: The Corey Hotline.

Instruments: Saxophone (mentored by the late Bleeding Gums Murphy), some guitar, and, one day perhaps, the accordion.

Original compositions: "That Same Ol' Red Dress Blues," "Puny Allowance Blues," "Pounded by the Dodgeball Blue and "I Been Good So Long, It Looks Like Bad to Me."

SHE'S GOT THE BRAINS AND TALENT TO GO AS FAR AS SHE WANTS. AND WHEN SHE DOES, I'LL BE RIGHT THERE TO BORROW MONEY.

In a cruel and heartless act of terror, Bart rips the head off of poor Mister Honeybunny in order to intimidate Lisa and cripple her ability to compete against him in the championship hockey game. This senseless act back fires when he realizes he has destroyed his own cherished childhood toy. Lisa drives the point home, taunting Bart by wearing the decapitated head on a chain around her neck during their big game.

Quote: "I wuv you!"

Description: Light blue fur, pink ears, crude stitching.

Ears: Floppy.

Texture: Fluffy.

Demeanor: Huggable.

Condition: Well-worn.

The innocence of youth (alas): Dressed in an elegant black suit and tie, Mister Honeybunny is more than just a comforting presence on scary nights. He's a remembrance of a gentler time—a time when a good night hug and a warm smile could send a child like Bart off to a land of lollipop dreams, a land of happy little elves and yummy ice cream, a land far removed from the competitive bloodlust and savage mayhem that is Pee Wee Hockey.

THE INTEL ON THIS ACTION JUST WASN'T UP TO SNUFF.

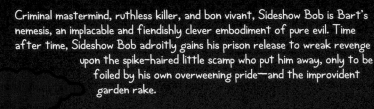

SIDESHOW BOB BART'S MORTAL ENEMY

Criminal mastermind, ruthless killer, and bon vivant, Sideshow Bob is Bart's nemesis, an implacable and fiendishly clever embodiment of pure evil. Time after time, Sideshow Bob adroitly gains his prison release to wreak revenge upon the spike-haired little scamp who put him away, only to be foiled by his own overweening pride—and the improvident garden rake.

Quote: "I did once try to kill the world's greatest lover, but then I realized there were laws against suicide."

Real name: Robert Underdunk Terwilliger

Musical likes: The Whimsical stylings of Gilbert & Sullivan

Musical dislikes: The Whimsical maundering of Gilbert O'Sullivan.

Potential Simpson Witness Relocation Sites: Cape Feare, Terror Lake, New Horrorfield, Screamville.

Suffers from: Over-articulation, or Long-word Pronouncing Syndrome, as it is seldom called.

Turn-ons: Buddha, The Republican Party, shad roe, and "Prison Bride Magazine."

Turn-offs: Television, Tom Clancy books, "MacGyver," and prison-issue shower sandals.

Awards: Daytime Emmy for "Sideshow Bob's Cavalcade of Whimsy."

INSIDE EVERY HARDENED CRIMINAL BEATS THE HEART OF A 10-YEAR-OLD BOY. AND VICE VERSA.

JESSICA LOVEJOY
SWEET & PERFECT MINISTER'S DAUGHTER WITH A HEART OF EVIL

The only daughter of Helen and the Reverend Timothy Lovejoy, Jessica Lovejoy craves attention—and what better way to attain it than by courting the Devil's cabana boy, Bart Simpson. With her pretty face and bad behavior, she bewitches Bart, who goes to incredible lengths to win her love—even making the supreme sacrifice of attending Sunday School.

Quote: "Do you ever think anything you don't say?"

Turn-ons: Pulling fire alarms, ultra-Xtreme skateboarding, and stealing from the collection plate.

Special skills: Baton twirling, toilet paper tossing, and making God's words sound plausible to Bart.

Grades: Straight "A"s.

Garments: Pretty in pink.

Expelled for: Building pipe-bombs, instigating glee club brawls, stealing from the School Chapel collection plate, and exploding toilets.

Hair: Long, black, luxurious, smells like red Froot Loops.

Signs that some poor sap is in love with her: Light-headedness, feelings of tension through the chestal area, improved hygiene, and strutting.

SHE'S LIKE A MILK DUD. SWEET ON THE OUTSIDE, POISON ON THE INSIDE.

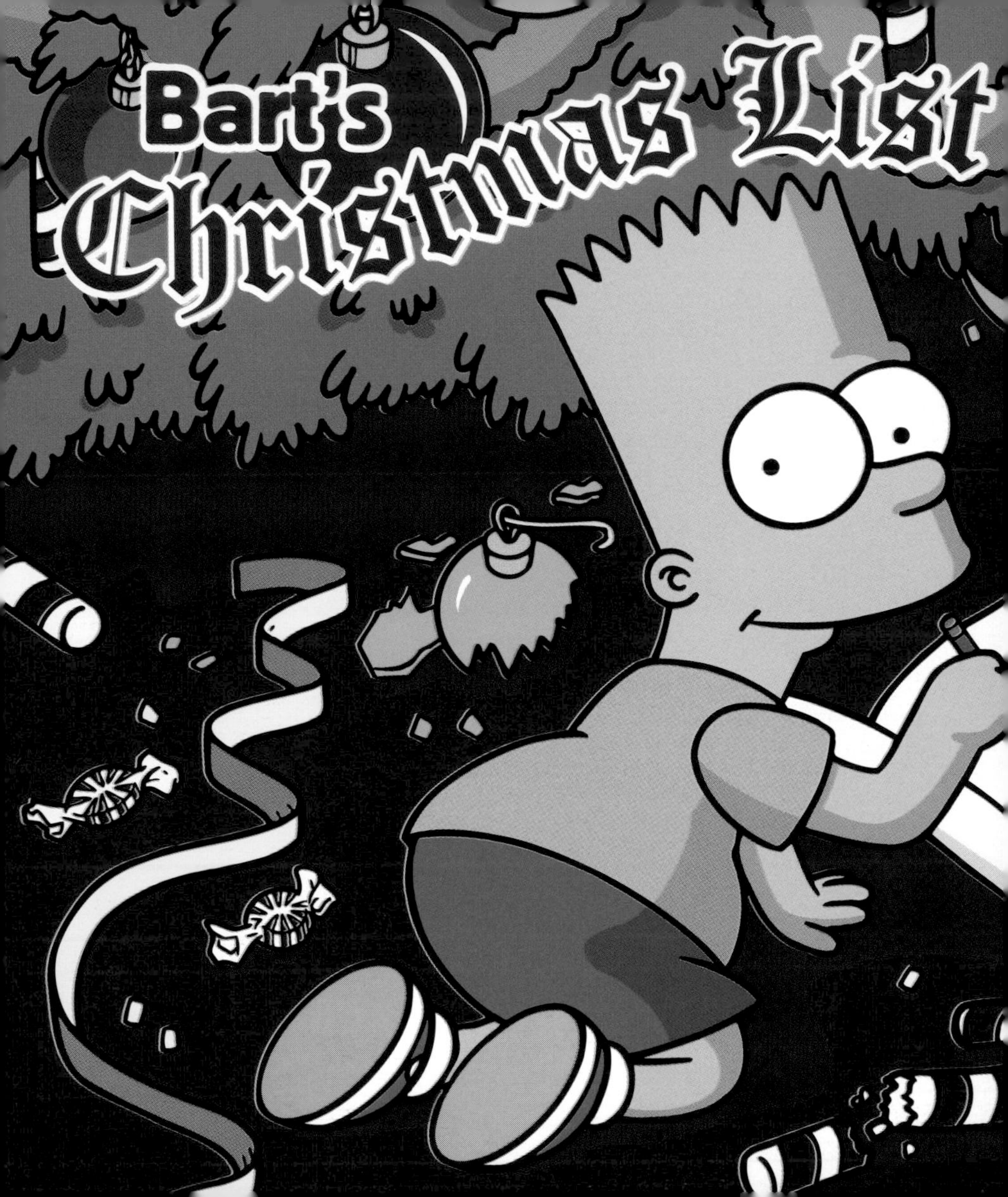
Bart's Christmas List

DEAR S-MAN,

I'D LIKE THE FOLLOWING ITEMS DELIVERED IN TIME FOR CHRISTMAS, WHICH FALLS ON DECEMBER 25th THIS YEAR.

- ☐ HOT PEPPER GUM (ENOUGH FOR EVERYONE).
- ☐ A NAKED LADY TATTOO.
- ☐ LITTLE SISTER REPELLANT.
- ☐ MY OWN PRIVATE ENTRANCE.
- ☐ A GOLD TOOTH (NOT GRAMPA'S).
- ☐ EVERY DVD EVER MADE.
- ☐ AIR CONDISHUNER IN TREE HOUSE.
- ☐ PHONY VAMPIRE FANGS.
- ☐ BUNS OF STEEL.
- ☐ SHIVERING CHIHUAHUA IN A TEACUP.
- ☐ ITCHY & SCRATCHY LAWN DARTS.
- ☐ BURGLAR ALARM IN BEDROOM.
- ☐ A MOON ROCK.

- ☐ EXTREME SPORTING GOODS.
- ☐ ELEVATOR SHOES.
- ☐ BONESTORM Ⅵ - THE BONENING.
- ☐ LI'L DUFFY HOME BREWERY KIT.
- ☐ THE ULTRA-RARE "RADIOACTIVE MAN/DONALD RUMSFELD CROSSOVER #1"
- ☐ SQUISHEE MACHINE FOR MY ROOM.
- ☐ STINKWEED.
- ☐ ROBOT BUTLER.
- ☐ RUBBER CEMENT FOR MAKING FAKE BOOGERS.
- ☐ BATPOLE FROM MY ROOM TO THE BASEMENT.
- ☐ WEDGIE-PROOF UNDER-PANTS.
- ☐ PEACE ON EARTH (IF YOU HAVE TIME).

P.S. I KNOW I HAVUNT BEEN GOOD THIS YEAR. BUT JUST REMEMBER, I KNOW WHERE YOU LIVE, MAN!

BART

BART'S RECIPES FOR

#74 - BARTENDER MERCIES

1. Call a local watering hole—any place with a bartender and a room full of raucous drunks will do.
2. Ask to speak to any of the following fictitious people:

- "Hal. Last name, Atosis."
- "Seymour. Last name, Butz."
- "Ivana. Last name, Kissyu"
- "Amanda. Last name, Huggenkiss."
  - "Anita. Last name, Bath."
  - "Hugh. Last name, Jass."
  - "Mike. Last name, Rotch."
  - "Ollie. Last name, Tabooger."

(Caution: Never say the first name and the last name together, or you risk tipping your hand!)

3. The unsuspecting sap on the other end of the line will shout out to his customers something like "Hey, has anyone seen Mike Rotch?" or "I'm looking for Amanda Huggenkiss!" or if you're lucky, "Hey everybody! Ollie Tabooger!"
4. Join the boozers on the other end of the line in fits of laughter at the expense of your patsy.

TELEPHONE FUN

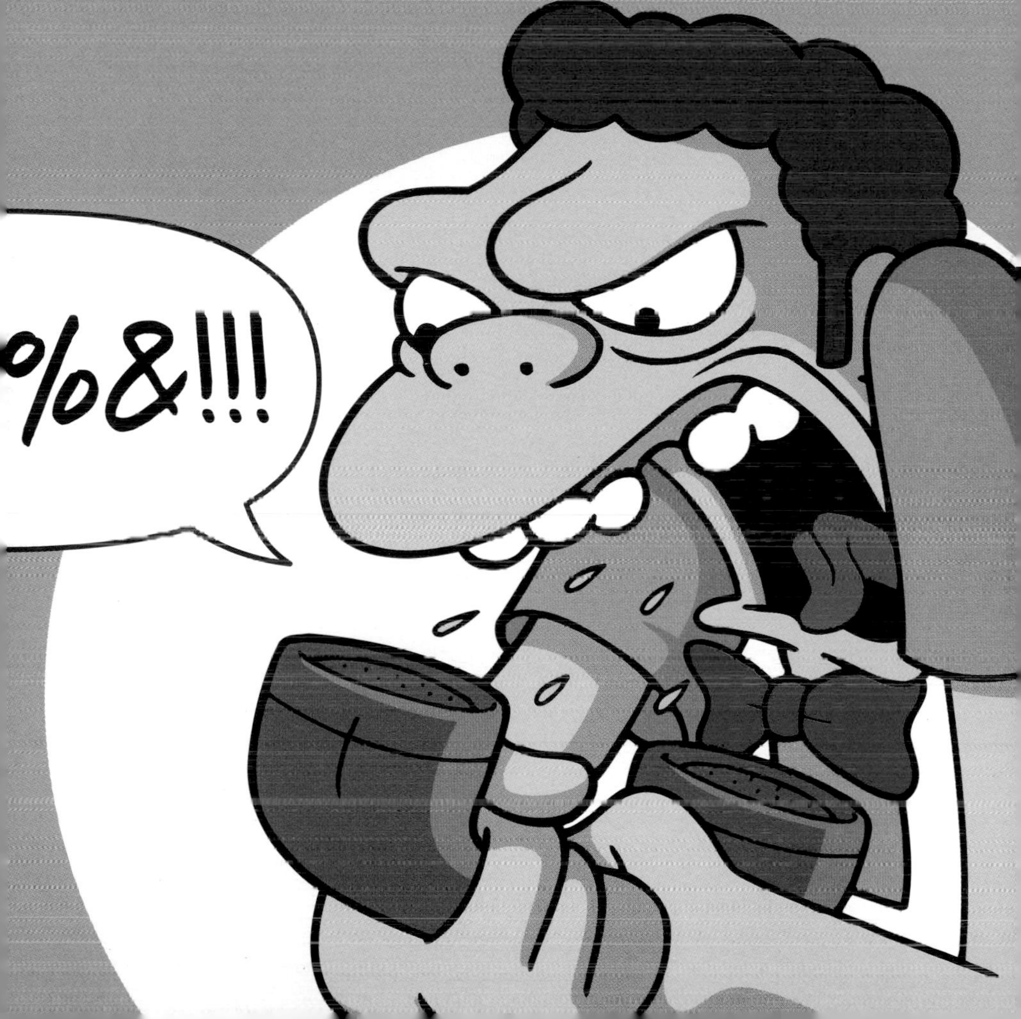
%&!!!

Where, oh where can a young boy go to be alone with his thoughts?

How about... BART SIMPSON'S DREAM TREEHOUSE!

1. The Bart Tower (fully equipped with model rocket defense system, telescopes, laser pointers, and salsa-filled water balloons).

2. Escalator to Bart Tower.

3. Itchy & Scratchy cartoons 24/7.

4. Jumbo mini-fridge.

5. The Bottled Treehouse of Kandor.

6. Pen archery corner.

7. Dunk tank w/ Skinner.

8. Hambone Alley - the designated hambone area in the treehouse!

9. Jacuzzi (with remote-controlled submarines).

10. Video projector (for watching TV on the side of the Flanders' house or Homer's stomach).

11. Bubblegum cigar humidor.

12. Waterslide.

13. Gabbo piñata.

14. Takeout menus.

15. Cupcake chandelier.

16. Carving station.

17. Squishee station.

18. Half pipe.

19. Milhouse crash area.

20. Pie-barrow (to throw at kids going down the waterslide).

21. Arcade (games include: Itchy & Scratchy Death Death Revolution, Big Rig JackKnifer, Innocent Bystander II, Shock and Awesome, and Underachiever).

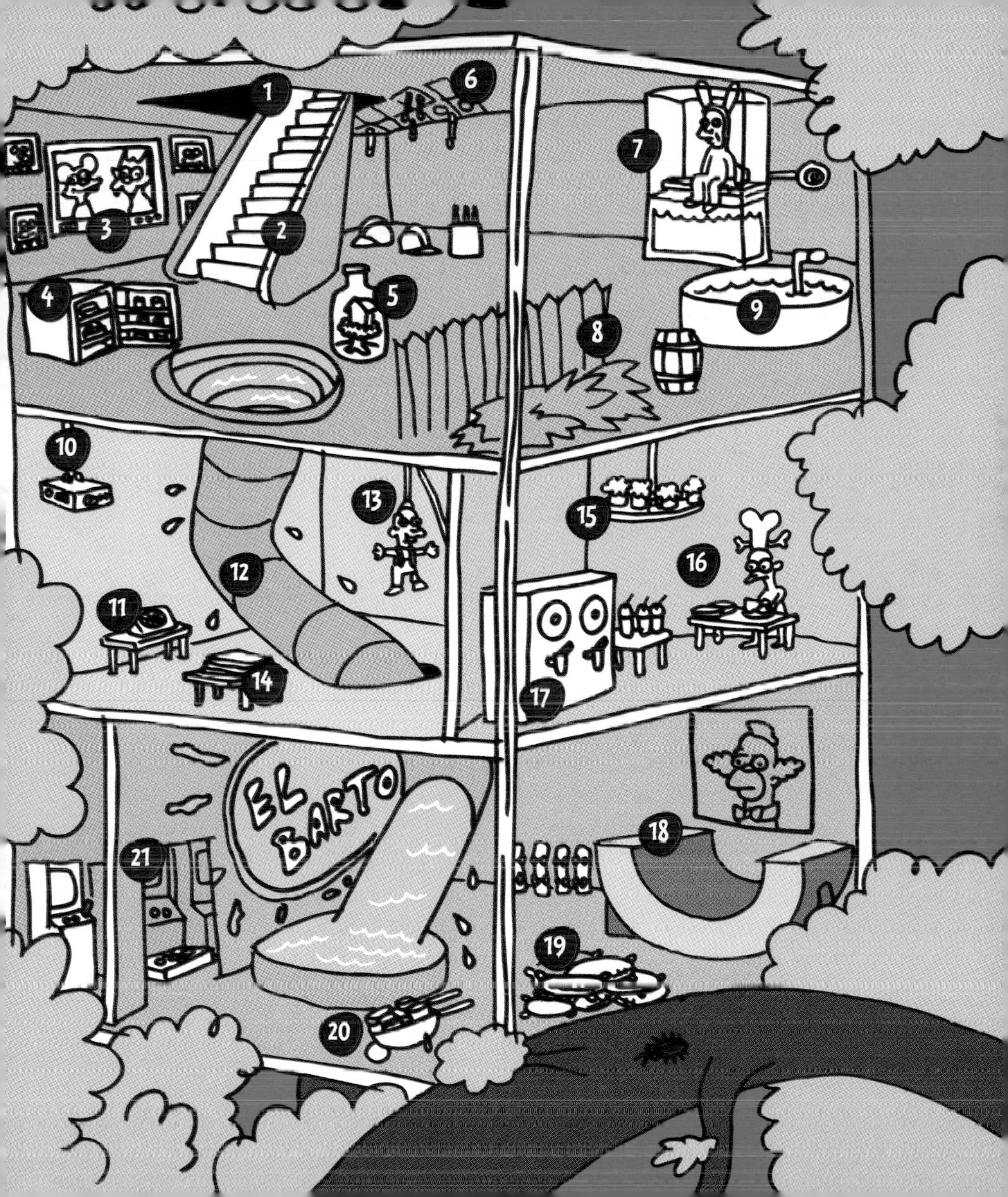
1
2
3
4
5
6
7
8
9
10
11
12
13
14
15
16
17
EL BARTO
18
19
20
21

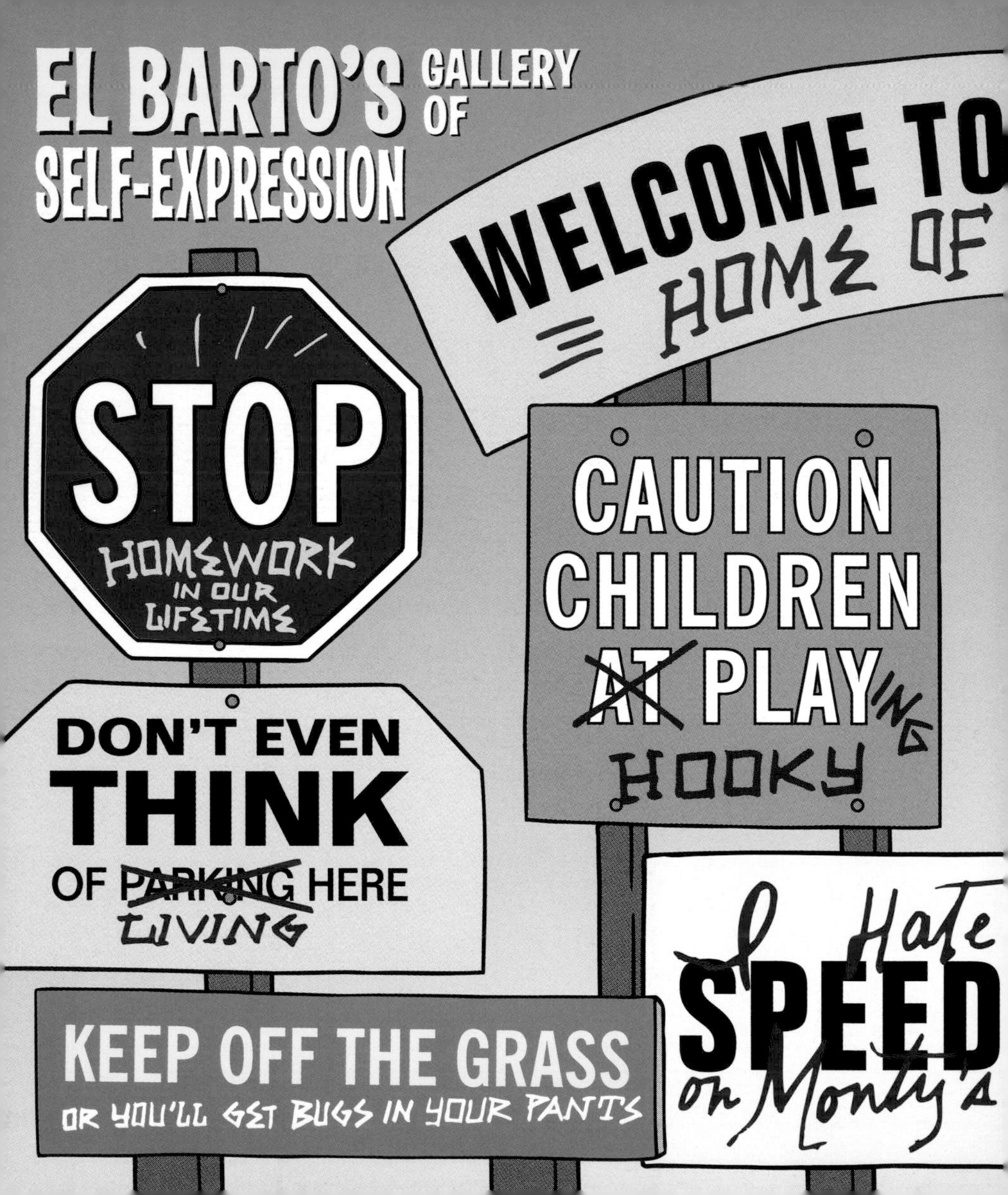
EL BARTO'S GALLERY OF SELF-EXPRESSION
WELCOME TO
HOME OF
STOP
HOMEWORK
IN OUR
LIFETIME
CAUTION
CHILDREN
~~AT~~ PLAYING
HOOKY
DON'T EVEN
THINK
OF ~~PARKING~~ HERE
LIVING
I Hate
SPEED
on Monty's
KEEP OFF THE GRASS
OR YOU'LL GET BUGS IN YOUR PANTS

SKINNER IS A DIP

SPRINGFIELD

EL BARTO!

PLEASE DRIVE FRIENDLY

& PUSH THE PEDAL TO THE METAL

IGNORE THIS SIGN AHEAD

No Yelling! FUN HERE!

that BUMP Nose

NO SMOKING! CROAKING

BART'S BOTTOM 40

1. Lisa's saxophone
2. The dreaded Rear Admiral
3. Wedgies
4. Wet Willies
5. Purple Nurples
6. Being caught red-handed
7. The hard crusty stuff on top of Mom's casseroles
8. The gooey glop underneath the hard crusty stuff on top of Mom's casseroles
9. Principal Skinner's secret file on me
10. The fact that Otto hardly ever lets me drive the school bus
11. Creamed corn (except as an ingredient in fake vomit)
12. Parents who have signatures that are really hard to forge
13. Accidentally feeling gum stuck underneath a restaurant table
14. Wrinkled old grown-ups—I hope I never become one
15. The cheap, lousy prizes that come in boxes of Frosted Krusty Klumps
16. Sucking on a pen at school and suddenly realizing that your mouth is full of ink
17. Vegetables that don't fly well off your spoon
18. The recurring nightmare that I'm a chip off the old block
19. Stories that end with a moral
20. Non-violent cartoons

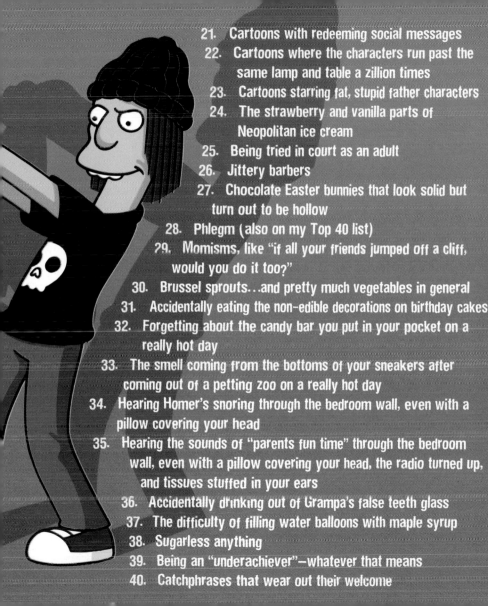

21. Cartoons with redeeming social messages
22. Cartoons where the characters run past the same lamp and table a zillion times
23. Cartoons starring fat, stupid father characters
24. The strawberry and vanilla parts of Neopolitan ice cream
25. Being tried in court as an adult
26. Jittery barbers
27. Chocolate Easter bunnies that look solid but turn out to be hollow
28. Phlegm (also on my Top 40 list)
29. Momisms, like "if all your friends jumped off a cliff, would you do it too?"
30. Brussel sprouts...and pretty much vegetables in general
31. Accidentally eating the non-edible decorations on birthday cakes
32. Forgetting about the candy bar you put in your pocket on a really hot day
33. The smell coming from the bottoms of your sneakers after coming out of a petting zoo on a really hot day
34. Hearing Homer's snoring through the bedroom wall, even with a pillow covering your head
35. Hearing the sounds of "parents fun time" through the bedroom wall, even with a pillow covering your head, the radio turned up, and tissues stuffed in your ears
36. Accidentally drinking out of Grampa's false teeth glass
37. The difficulty of filling water balloons with maple syrup
38. Sugarless anything
39. Being an "underachiever"—whatever that means
40. Catchphrases that wear out their welcome

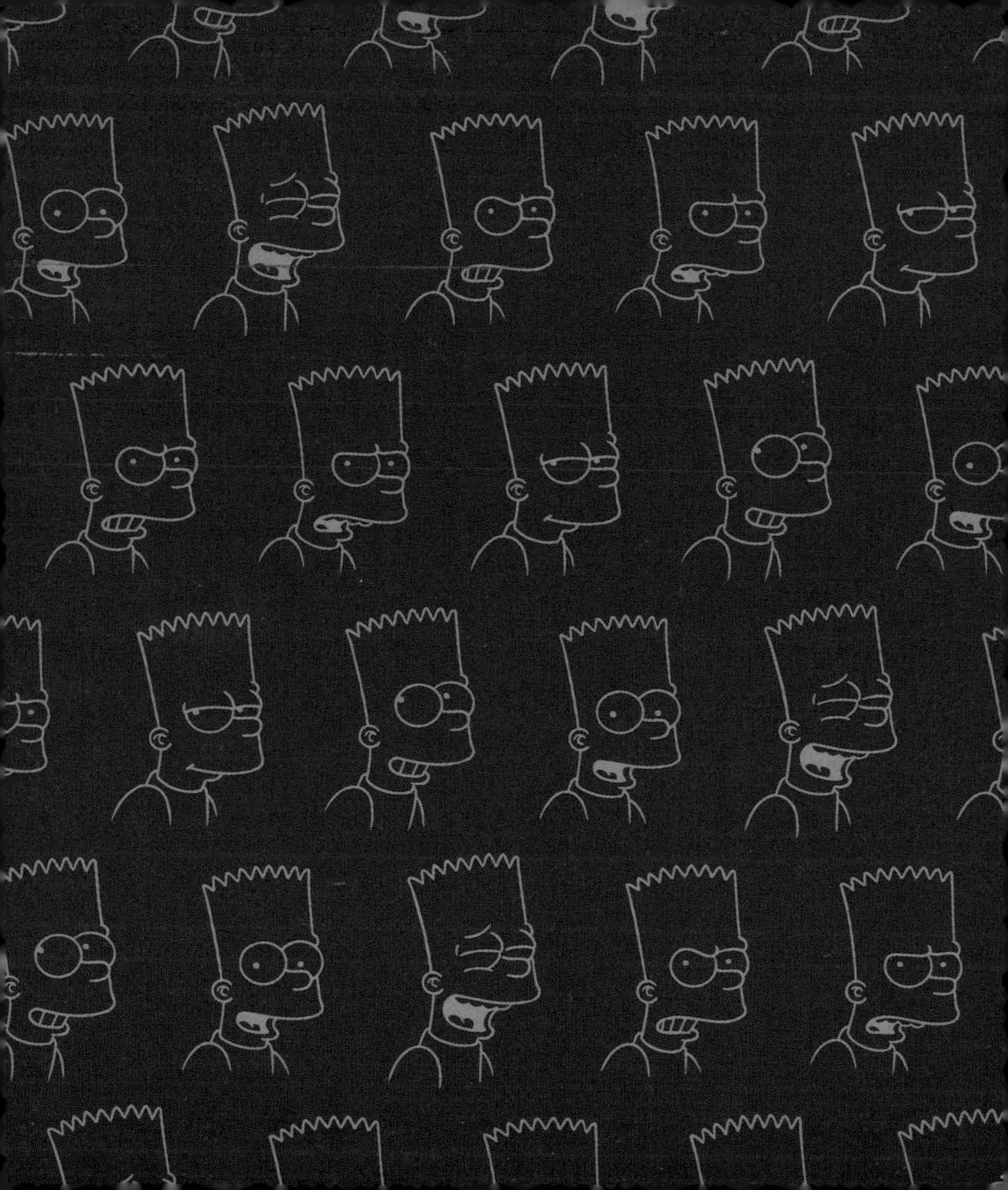